Reiki

Healing energy for mind, body and spirit

Reiki

Healing energy for mind, body and spirit

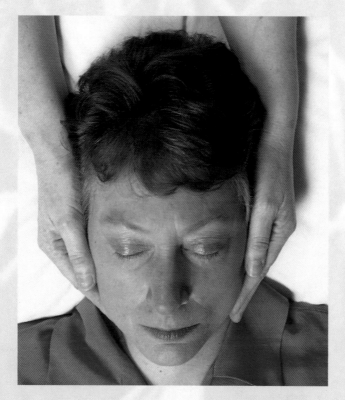

Charmian Winser

D&S
BOOKS

First published in 2001 by D&S Books

© 2001 D&S Books

D&S Books
Cottage Meadow, Bocombe,
Parkham, Bideford
Devon, England
EX39 5PH

e-mail us at:-
enquiries.dspublishing@care4free.net

This edition printed 2001

ISBN 1-903327-09-1

Editorial Director: Sarah King
Editor: Judith Millidge
Project Editor: Clare Haworth-Maden
Photographer: Paul Forrester
Designer: 2H Design

Distributed in the UK & Ireland by
Bookmart Limited
Desford Road
Enderby
Leicester LE9 5AD

Distributed in Australia by
Herron Books
39 Commercial Road
Fortitude Valley
Queensland 4006

1 3 5 7 9 10 8 6 4 2

Contents

Introduction

REIKI

(pronounced 'ray-key') is an ancient form of hands-on healing, thought to be thousands of years old. It was rediscovered by Dr Mikao Usui, a Japanese gentleman, early in the 20th century.

The word 'Reiki' is usually translated as 'universal life force'. Reiki can be learnt by anyone, regardless of faith or age, although it is not recommended for children under the age of seven.

- Reiki helps to restore balance within the body.
- Reiki is holistic. It works on mind, body and spirit.
- Reiki is very simple to learn and to apply.

Anyone can learn Reiki

Reiki has spread around the world at an astonishing speed. It is the fastest-growing form of hands-on healing anywhere. One reason for this is its simplicity. All that you need to know in order to treat yourself or your friends and family can be taught in a class of two days or so. Another reason for its popularity is that it is so enjoyable. It de-stresses, and it detoxifies painlessly. It fills the person with glowing energy and calm.

During a treatment, Reiki pours through the body of the giver and out through his or her hands into the body of the recipient. This manifests itself as a feeling of warmth or tingling.

Clients are normally asked to commit to three or four daily treatments of Reiki, with follow-up treatments as necessary. This gives time for the energy to act on the root of the problem and to work deeply on the body.

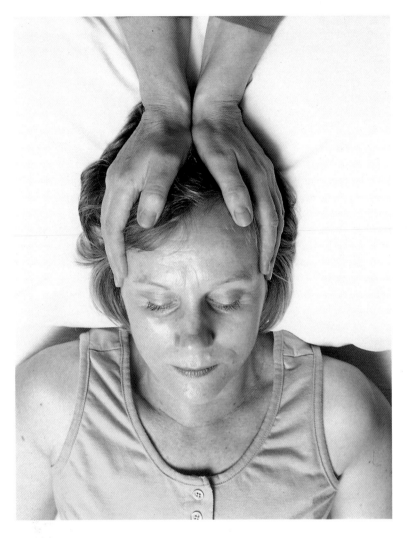

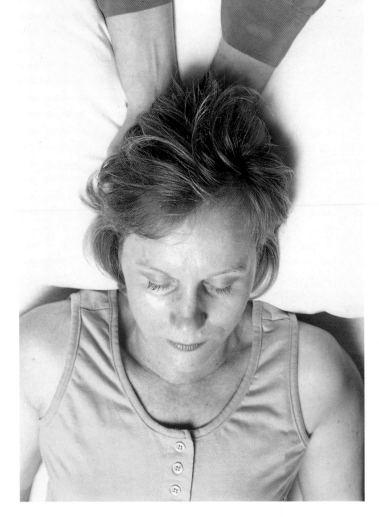

Reiki is a holistic form of hands-on healing that rebalances the body, mind and spirit.

During treatment, Reiki works on many levels, rebalancing the whole mind, body and spirit. The energy is experienced as deeply relaxing and very soothing. People often find that their thoughts slow down or stop, and that they drift into a deep state or even fall asleep.

It is not necessary to believe that Reiki will work for you. It just does. It does not require faith. Children respond well to Reiki. You cannot give too much Reiki. The energy simply stops when the person has received all that is required.

Reiki is split into three levels or degrees. This book contains many of the basics that you would learn in a Level I class and gives a short explanation of the other two levels.

Note
It must be stressed that this is simply a guide to what Reiki might achieve; it will not necessarily relieve symptoms or eradicate them. Reiki is not a substitute for a properly qualified doctor, and no medicines should be discontinued without the advice of a medical professional. It is illegal in the UK for children to be treated by a practitioner without the written consent of a parent or guardian.

The history of Reiki

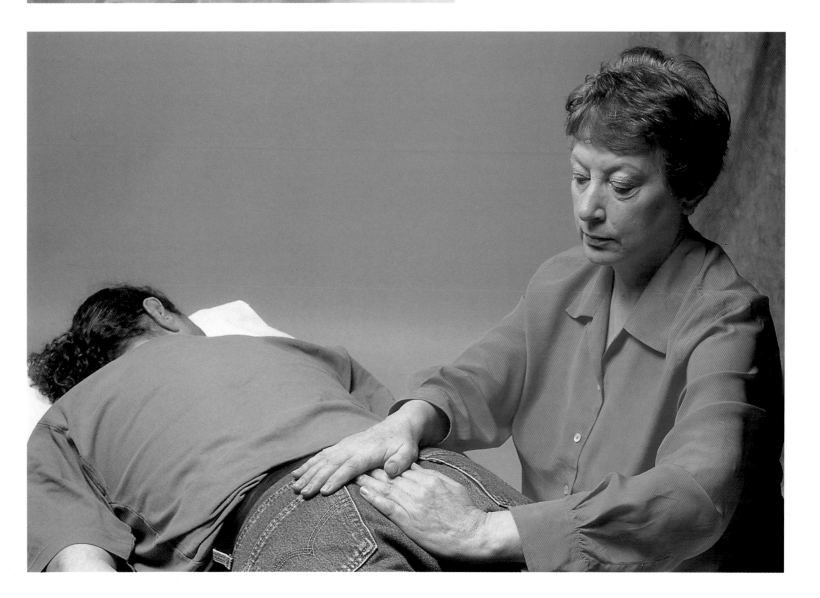

Until the late 1990s, all we knew of the origins of Reiki came from Hawayo Takata, the woman who introduced it to the USA just after the Second World War. She had wisely altered some of the details in order to make Reiki acceptable to a predominantly Christian country.

Some of the following information has been taken from the memorial erected to Dr Usui. It lies in the grounds of the Saihoji Temple, Tokyo. The *Usui Reiki Ryoho Gakkai* (Usui Reiki Healing Society), which was founded by Dr Usui during his lifetime, erected it shortly after his death. The society still exists today.

Dr Mikao Usui was born on 15 August 1864 in southern Japan. He was apparently a businessman who had suffered a reversal of fortune. He meditated diligently. At some point, he carried out an extended fast on Mount Kurama, just outside Kyoto, and felt the energy that he was later to call Reiki flow into him.

He opened a clinic in Tokyo in 1921 and, after helping many victims of the great Tokyo earthquake of 1923, his fame spread. By the time that he died, on 9 March 1926, he had over 2,000 students. Dr Usui gave a few of his students the ability to pass on this remarkable energy. Among them was a reserve naval officer named Dr Chujiro Hayashi.

Western origins

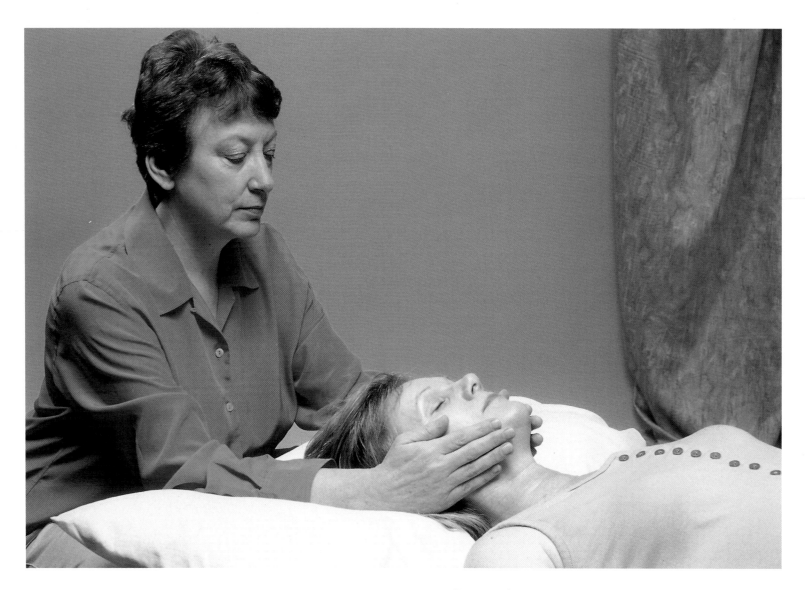

A dynamic, diminutive Japanese woman brought Reiki to the West. Her name was Hawayo Takata.

Hawayo Takata was born into a Japanese community in Hawaii on Christmas Eve 1900. In 1930 her husband died, aged only 34. Left alone to provide for her two daughters, she worked extremely hard and became very ill, suffering a nervous breakdown. In 1935, just when she felt that things could not get any worse, her sister died.

It was her duty to return to Japan in order to inform her parents. She also hoped that she would be able to rest and receive treatment for her illness. In Tokyo, a doctor diagnosed a tumour, among other ills, and ordered her to gain weight before he would operate. She became convinced that she did

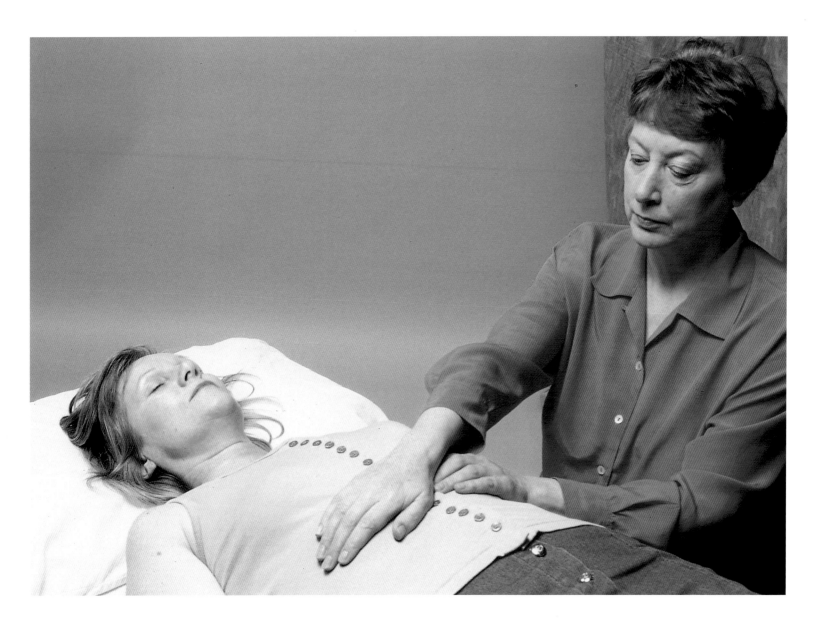

not need the operation, and asked if there was any other way that she might be cured. The surgeon hesitated, and then said that he knew of a healer who had a clinic in Tokyo. His wife was a student of this healing method, and she took her along.

So, early in 1936, Hawayo Takata met Dr Chujiro Hayashi and experienced Reiki for the first time.

She made a remarkable recovery and eventually persuaded Dr Hayashi to teach her. Under his guidance, for a whole year she gave treatments every day. By the summer of 1937 she had been given second-degree Reiki and was able to return to Hawaii to practise Reiki.

Shortly afterwards, Dr Hayashi visited Hawaii. He gave talks and demonstrations and taught Reiki. Before he returned to Japan several months later, he made Hawayo Takata the first person outside Japan to become a Reiki master, qualified to teach, as well as to practise, Reiki.

By the time that Hawayo Takata died, in December 1980, she had taught Reiki not only on Hawaii, but all over North, and much of Central, America. She had created 22 Reiki masters.

What is Reiki?

Nowadays, there must scarcely be a region where someone does not have Reiki. It is taught and practised in Indian ashrams and Western clinics alike. This is testament indeed to a remarkable energy.

Why is Reiki so popular?

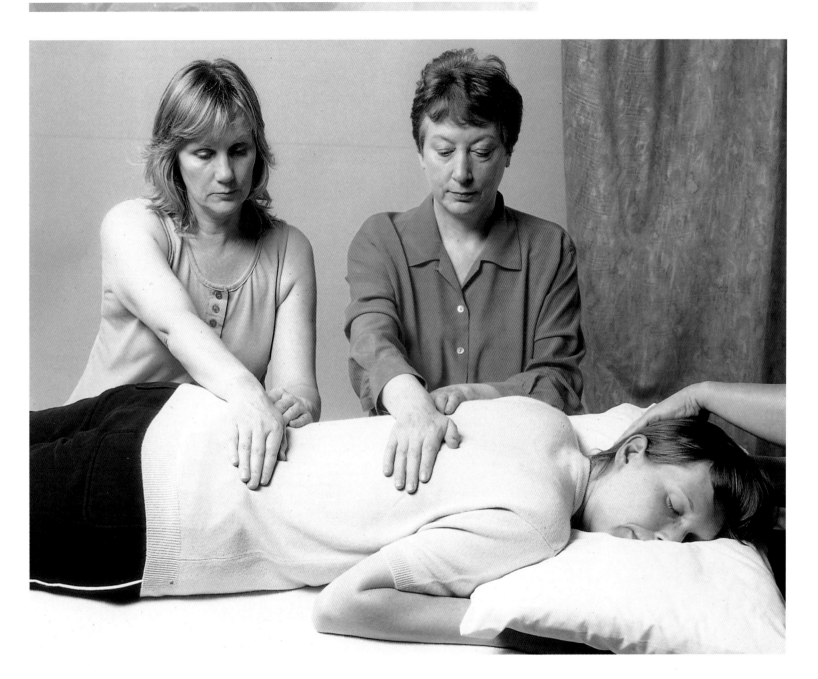

It is because it is very easy to pass on. All that you need to know in order to heal your friends and family is taught in a Level I class. The class usually takes place over two or two-and-a-half days, or over four sessions of approximately four hours. You should be reasonably confident by the end of the class that Reiki is working in your hands. A good teacher will give you follow-up advice.

Reiki is not a cure-all. It is an aid. It does not replace the medical profession. You must never cease taking medication without consulting your doctor. However, Reiki may ease your symptoms and even put them into full remission. Many health professionals have themselves learnt Reiki. Indeed, one Reiki master of my acquaintance, who was a teacher of nurses, was encouraged to share her knowledge of complementary therapies in her place of work.

Reiki can speed recovery from illness, trauma and surgery. Hospitals are now used to requests from visitors for permission to give hands-on healing to their patients. Indeed, although it is courteous to ask, by law they cannot refuse.

In both giving and receiving, Reiki works both ways. The recipient knows consciously or subconsciously what he or she needs and Reiki pours in to fill that need. Reiki is deeply relaxing. Usually, by the time that the first three or four hand positions have been completed, all chat has ceased from even the most hyperactive person.

Reiki kanji

Studying the Japanese pictograms (*kanjis*) of Reiki gives some fascinating insights into the meaning and power of Reiki.

Kanjis are pictorial representations, a little like hieroglyphics. They represent concepts of the spoken word. Each brushstroke, or series of brushstrokes, represents an idea. The most usual version of the Reiki *kanji* that you may see advertised is the one shown on page 6. The version on this page is in the old Bushido script. It shows the concepts of Reiki more clearly.

The upper pictogram is the word *rei*. The top line represents heaven. The vertical line coming down from it is drawing heaven's energy down. The brushstrokes surrounding the vertical line denote clouds and rain. The three boxes represent mouths. Three mouths mean prayer. The next line also symbolises heaven, with a vertical line bringing heaven's energy down, this time to the earth, shown by the bottom line. The little upturned 'Vs' in between are dancing shamans (priests). Thus the whole upper pictogram shows the power of heaven raining down to earth through the power of prayer, priesthood and ritual.

The lower pictogram is the word *ki*. The first three brushstrokes of the lower pictogram represent mist. The next brushstroke, with its sweeping tail, depicts the sun's rays beaming down to earth. The remainder represents rice, with its stalk, leaves and roots, growing in the paddy field. The word *ki* translates as 'energy' or 'life force'.

The whole lower *kanji* shows the cycle of energy: fire, earth, air and water. The roots of the rice are planted in the soil. The mist rises from the water through the power of the sun. The rice grows through being nourished by the sun, earth, air and water in an endless cycle of energy.

The most popular translation of the word Reiki is 'universal life force'. In fact, this is an injustice. The energy of *rei* is beyond the universe, beyond thought and form. It is the transcendent spiritual essence out of which the universe springs. It is enlightenment or nirvana. Thus, alternative translations might be 'spiritual life force' or 'enlightenment energy'.

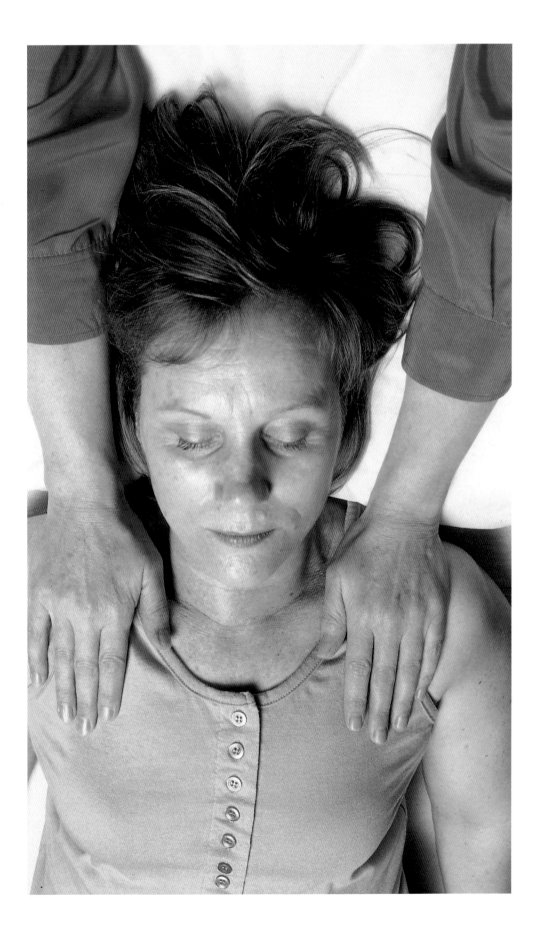

Some people do not understand what Reiki is, even after reading a book on the subject. There are reasons for this.

Firstly, you need to experience Reiki in order to understand it. It is no use telling someone what it is like to fall in love. They will never understand until it happens. The person who has been attuned to Reiki has the daily experience of warm hands and of feeling Reiki sink into the body, releasing tensions and calming the emotions and mind.

Secondly, remember the translation of Reiki: 'universal life force'. This life force is present everywhere. It is intangible, but felt. Every creature has it; it is in every blade of grass. After the rain, the earth feels refreshed and more alive.

When someone feels on top of the world, we remark that he or she seems to glow. This is because the person is full of life. The person who is habitually full of life is rarely ill.

The Reiki principles

Dr Usui formulated five Reiki principles, which he would ask his students to recite at each class.

Reiki is not just a physical treatment. It is a personal and spiritual growth therapy. It teaches you to take responsibility for yourself. Each time that you give yourself a treatment or receive a treatment, Reiki is not only healing your body, but also your mind and spirit. It behoves us to take responsibility for what we are creating. Disease is often not simply physical in origin. Its roots may, for instance, lie in anxiety and depression. As we learn to understand more about our psyches, we begin to realise that our attitudes play a large part in the structure of our lives. If our attitude is positive, we attract positive people and events. When we are full of doubt, we fail to seize our opportunities.

It is no easy thing to be positive when our upbringing is the reverse. But this is precisely when our mettle is being tested. We are meant to grow. Will we face the challenge? Will we seize the opportunity and make a success of our lives?

Nowadays there are many opportunities to grow through our social conditioning; there is a plethora of self-growth courses; the media presents ways of helping us to grow into an awareness of ourselves and our world. Taboos are bravely faced and, sometimes after a period of resistance, we congratulate them for bringing these issues to our consciousness and helping us to understand.

Reiki helps us to grow through our conditioning. When we put our hands on ourselves, we submit to the 'infinite intelligence' that is guiding Reiki to free our bodies and psyches from their difficulties and to face the fears and assumptions that limit us.

Reiki principles

Just for today . . .

do not worry

do not get angry

show your gratitude

be honest

honour every living thing

If we feel overburdened by life, we need to take a break.

Just for today . . . do not worry

Anxiety is such a common form of stress that our bodies are constantly submitted to a bombardment of tensions that make our muscles seize up. Reiki is a wonderful relaxant and tonic after a stressful day.

But what is causing the stress? What are we worrying about? Is it pressure of work, the children's attitudes or a personal weakness? Whatever it is, Reiki can help to resolve it.

The opposite of worry is trust. Faith in the future or faith in life is not easy to find when you are under great duress. But, again, that is precisely when your faith can be tested.

It is virtually impossible to go through life without anxiety. Only the greatest saints can be so detached. Reiki does not ask you never to worry. It asks you to trust. It also invites you to look at what is causing you to worry. The worry and pain of the terminal illness of a close relative is not going to go away. Reiki will considerably relieve it and will help you to let go.

Worrying about what people think of us is often a much more deep-rooted problem. It stems from lack of self-esteem. Ask Reiki to help you. You can also put your hands on yourself if you are

an atheist and invite your psyche to heal your self-doubt. Equally, you can ask any spiritual being to help. It does not matter who or what you invoke. It is the intention that counts.

When we whole-heartedly want something, we draw it towards us. But we are often half-hearted about our needs because we are full of apprehension. Is it selfish? Will I be able to do it? Perhaps we feel that there are too many hurdles in the way. So we go through life only half-trying, or give up on our dreams because we feel that they are unrealistic.

Worry is fear and doubt, our inability to trust each other or ourselves. Whilst we can be exhorted to trust life, God or Reiki, very few of us would automatically trust another human being. We need to *earn* the trust that is put in us. When others cause us to worry, we need to look at exactly what we can do about it and leave the rest. Let go. It is not easy. We must let others make their own mistakes and learn from them. Once we face the thing that we fear, it often turns out to have no foundation.

The constant exhortation on the spiritual path is to let go. Let go of your attachments and resistance.

Just for today . . . do not get angry

Anger is a tool. The trouble is that we too often use it as a weapon.

We may feel angry because we feel threatened, because our boundaries have been crossed, or our sense of honour, or our sense of justice, is outraged. These are valid reasons. Again, the trouble is that sometimes our boundaries have been breached on so many occasions that we have what therapists call a 'trigger point'. By now, we feel so threatened that we explode at the first whiff of a further breach. Such anger is not wrong. It simply needs to be addressed and healed.

Another major reason for anger is that our needs have not been met. Too often, men and women give their all to work, marriage and children, taking so little in return that they are desperate. You must make sure that you have sufficient time and attention for your needs. Giving yourself a half-hour Reiki treatment, or exchanging one, is a wonderful way to restore the balance.

Shortness of money is a terrible trigger point. The endless grind of living on the dole is an insult to one's dignity. There is little to be done when there is no work locally and little chance of living elsewhere. Such times have to be seen out somehow.

All of the above are valid reasons to feel so stressed that it boils over into anger. However, there are many other reasons for being angry that are not quite so valid. Sometimes we want our own way; sometimes our anger is a smoke screen to hide our discomfort because we know that we are wrong; sometimes we do not want to look at the truth; sometimes we are convinced that it is the other person's fault and sometimes we are good at blaming. A good argument makes us feel justified in holding onto our viewpoint. We do not have to give in and feel that our pride has been hurt.

We all get angry for the wrong reasons. Reiki invites us to look at our anger and ask for healing. We can have a treatment specifically for a problem. We can ask for help and insight. Level II Reiki provides powerful tools to help us.

Reiki is not asking us to repress our anger. That is very dangerous. It is better to put our hands on ourselves and ask what it is that we are learning. Is it to stand up for ourselves? Is it a stubborn attitude? Is it overtiredness? If we stay with our feelings and address them honestly, we may gain a valuable insight.

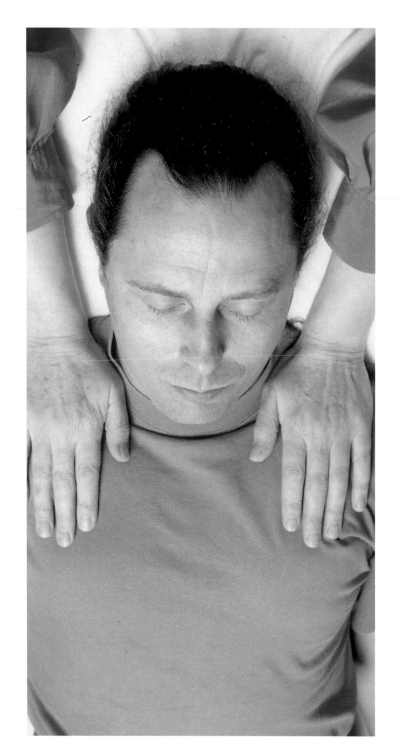

The constant exhortation of the spiritual path is to let go. Relax.

Just for today . . . show your gratitude

It does not cost much to put up your hand in acknowledgement of the driver who has just stopped to allow you to cross the road. It makes both you and the driver feel better. You feel grateful and he feels that he has done a good turn. Your spirits are lifted.

It is extraordinary how Reiki fills us full of gratitude, but this is one of its attributes. One person after another who has learnt Reiki will tell you how grateful they feel for receiving it. This is not only because they have been given the power to heal themselves. It is because it is part of the nature of Reiki. Gratitude fills us with love, and love is another intrinsic aspect of Reiki.

Constantly complaining about your problems does not help. It is better to do something constructive. A cheerful, positive attitude helps you to count your blessings. If we feel overburdened by life, then we need to take a break, to take stock of what we are doing. It is no use forcing yourself onwards: this kills gratitude. Find something, a hobby or new friends, give some time to a charity, which can be enormous fun, or involve your friends and family in a project.

Every time that I give someone Reiki I feel full of gratitude. I feel so privileged to work with this energy. This is a common response.

We have so much to be grateful for. When we take things for granted and then go through a bad time, we often look back in regret to better times. It is often better to recognise the lessons that we are learning and to grow, and eventually we may be grateful for the experience.

Just for today . . . be honest

Dishonesty removes our integrity. We cannot look *ourselves* in the face. We may bury some minor infractions inside, but our conscience knows, and we feel guilty. Eventually the hardened criminal and ruthless businessman forget to feel guilty, but the price is that they are out of touch with their finer feelings.

Reiki, so full of love, opens our hearts and brings us face to face with our guilt. What are we to do about it? The first step may be to ask for forgiveness. If that is not possible, then we must learn the lesson and forgive ourselves.

When we look within, we find many ways in which we are not true to ourselves. We may not ask for our needs to be met, we may not face a friend with an unkindness, we may push others. We need to rediscover ourselves.

The process of self-discovery is one of unfolding layer after layer of resistance, unresolved feelings and unexpected abilities. We bury inside us everything that we feel is unacceptable, or that we have been told is unacceptable. Some of the surprises are delightful. Eventually we come to the core of our being, but it is a long process. The greatest problem in unfolding ourselves is fear. We fear that we are not good enough, that we must face our sins. Actually, at the root of our being is such a great and glorious self that we are often afraid of facing it in case we seem egotistical.

The first hurdle to be faced may be the feeling of selfishness in trying to discover ourselves. We are taught that we must think of others before ourselves. We imagine that we may develop spiritually by selfless service to humankind. We may. But a doormat is not a very useful member of the community. Such a person rarely reflects back to others where they are going wrong. In order to be a fully functioning human being, we must face our demons and have the strength of character to fight for what is right.

Self-discovery means being honest enough to face ourselves as we are.

Just for today . . . honour every living thing

We have a completely different viewpoint on life from a century ago. Our viewpoint has become global. Two hundred years ago, it was not unusual for villagers to go no further than the nearest town during a whole lifetime. There was little concept of the world at large. Since the advent of space exploration, we have the pictures of our whole planet before our eyes. The awe of the astronauts who walked on the moon was tangible to us all; it was a spiritual experience and they returned changed men. The media uses satellite pictures of the earth constantly because it knows how fascinating they seem.

What makes them so interesting? On one level they expand our minds to a cosmic viewpoint, a mental leap only equalled by Copernicus nearly 500 years ago when he discovered that the earth went round the sun.

In the spiritual journey, there comes a time when the aspirant's consciousness starts to flip out to a wider perspective. The consciousness literally becomes global. The whole planet is experienced from outside. No longer is the human being seeing the world from within it, but a greater self is watching the human going through the motions of life on the planet. There are whole courses devoted to helping people to experience this expansion of consciousness.

A natural outflow of this change of viewpoint is the realisation that the earth is a living entity. It becomes impossible not to honour every living thing.

Preparation and attunements

While it is wonderful to receive a Reiki treatment, there comes a time when many people wish to learn to do it for themselves. Reiki should not be entered into as a business proposition. Whilst it is perfectly permissible to undertake Levels I and II with a view to practising Reiki professionally, be aware that if you have already been working for some time on your personal and spiritual growth, you should have a minimum of one year's experience of Reiki. If you have little or no experience of personal and spiritual growth, you should have two years' experience of Reiki before attempting to practise it professionally.

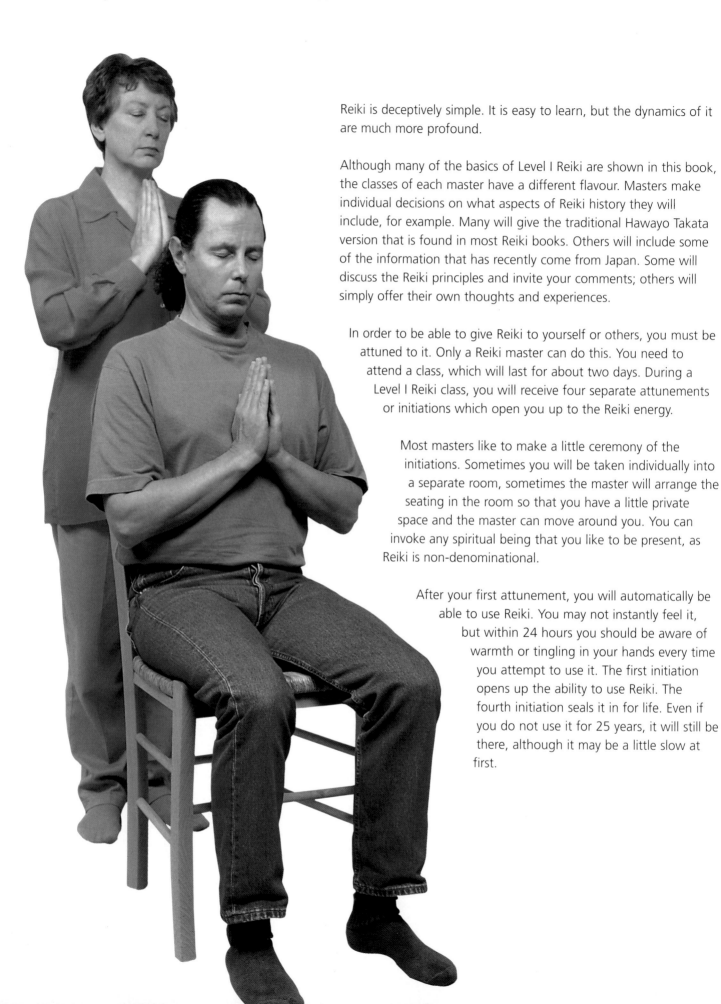

Reiki is deceptively simple. It is easy to learn, but the dynamics of it are much more profound.

Although many of the basics of Level I Reiki are shown in this book, the classes of each master have a different flavour. Masters make individual decisions on what aspects of Reiki history they will include, for example. Many will give the traditional Hawayo Takata version that is found in most Reiki books. Others will include some of the information that has recently come from Japan. Some will discuss the Reiki principles and invite your comments; others will simply offer their own thoughts and experiences.

In order to be able to give Reiki to yourself or others, you must be attuned to it. Only a Reiki master can do this. You need to attend a class, which will last for about two days. During a Level I Reiki class, you will receive four separate attunements or initiations which open you up to the Reiki energy.

Most masters like to make a little ceremony of the initiations. Sometimes you will be taken individually into a separate room, sometimes the master will arrange the seating in the room so that you have a little private space and the master can move around you. You can invoke any spiritual being that you like to be present, as Reiki is non-denominational.

After your first attunement, you will automatically be able to use Reiki. You may not instantly feel it, but within 24 hours you should be aware of warmth or tingling in your hands every time you attempt to use it. The first initiation opens up the ability to use Reiki. The fourth initiation seals it in for life. Even if you do not use it for 25 years, it will still be there, although it may be a little slow at first.

Attending a class will give you plenty of experience of using Reiki on yourself and others, which will build your confidence. The master and your classmates will provide feedback on how your hands feel. During the following three to four weeks, your energy system will be adapting to the attunements. It is quite important that you give yourself a daily treatment during this period. Thereafter, your mind and body will continue to adjust to the energy and grow.

The difference in your energy after receiving Reiki can be quite dramatic. People seem to glow more. Continuing your daily treatment after the first few weeks simply keeps building health and the regeneration of mind, body and spirit.

The initiations themselves seem to create changes in people. Sometimes the change is obvious during the class or immediately afterwards. Reactions to the attunements can vary considerably. Some people feel very little during the class and others experience a major change. Habits may die, insights may be gained and attitudes may alter. You may not realise for some considerable time after the class that a problem has disappeared until you trace it back to the class. There may be other effects. It is not unknown for people to become vegetarian after the class, or simply to lose the taste for coffee, tea or wine.

The changes that occur after a Level I initiation are usually pleasant or not too uncomfortable. If a person has done a great deal of work on him- or herself, Reiki may challenge him or her more or remove a bigger issue. Generally, some grace is given. After all, you are sitting in on two days of Reiki energy!

After you have been doing Reiki for a few months, you may feel drawn to taking a second-degree class. In your Level II class, you will receive either one or two initiations, depending on which stream of Reiki your master comes from.

At Level II, the energy can bite deeper and you may experience depression or some other adverse reaction. This is quite normal and should not be anything to worry about. I always encourage students to phone me if they are becoming concerned. But this more advanced level can give you a bigger grace, too. You may feel euphoric for several days, or you may go through a period of feeling wonderful, followed

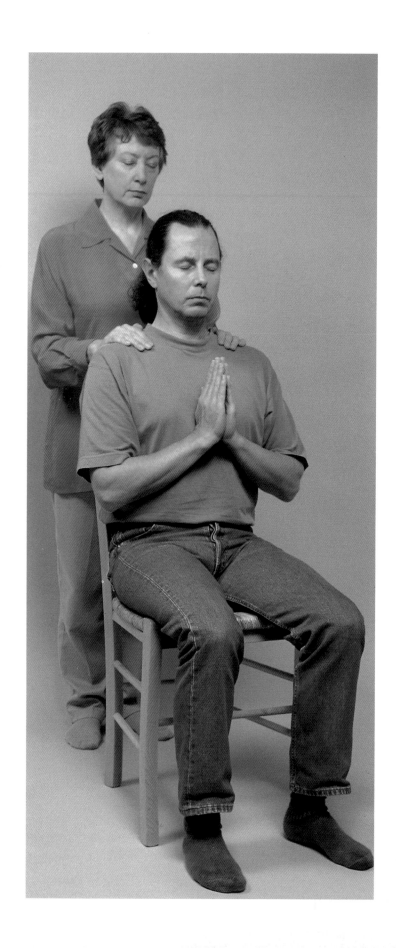

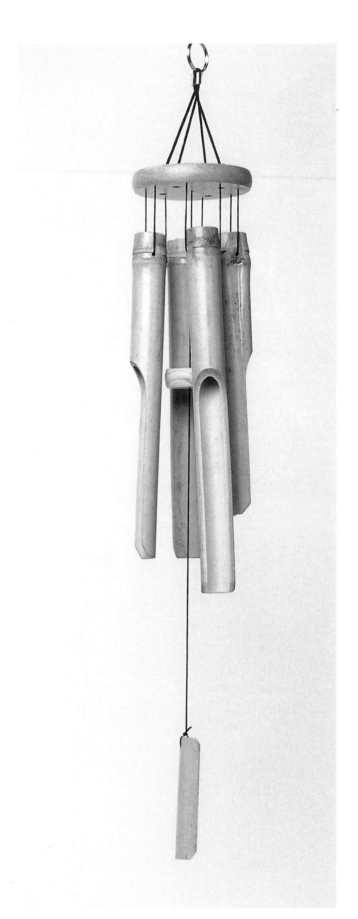

by the opposite. As at Level I, there are many possible reactions, and I encourage my students to share their concerns with me after the class.

Level III is the master level of training. During the whole period of training, which is roughly a year, the trainee undergoes profound changes. Issues will be raised and the trainee will be challenged to grow. It is not for the faint-hearted. Level III is a full spiritual path. It should not be entered into without understanding the implications of such a step.

Hawayo Takata's

injunction to her students

was, 'First Reiki yourself!'

Or, to use the ancient maxim,

'Physician, heal thyself'.

After being attuned to Reiki at any of the three levels, it is important to make time for a self-treatment every day for the first three weeks. Thereafter, students are recommended to Reiki themselves every day, and for the practitioner and master it is an obligation, although I do not think that anyone regards it as a chore!

Although it is preferable to set aside a certain time each day for self-treatment, you can actually give yourself unobtrusive doses throughout the day. You can do many of the hand positions on a train or bus. You can sit at the desk with your head in your hands whilst reading a document, you can self-treat with one hand while you are on the phone and you can relax in front of the television or read a book and enjoy Reiki at the same time.

Daily self-treatment becomes such a habit that we are often not conscious that we are doing it. The truth is that although you are given a solid format of hand positions to use as a full treatment, your hands take on a life of their own after a while, and you suddenly realise that they are flowing energy into some part or other. You go to bed and your hands might go onto your heart, or you wake in the middle of the night and they are on your head. You can be in the street and one hand is giving Reiki to your stomach.

When you are giving yourself Reiki, you may be aware that thoughts and feelings are arising. Reiki is working on transforming your consciousness, as well as your body. Issues from the past may arise, long-forgotten memories, embarrassments, fears. You may see colours, you may go into a deep state and become completely unaware of your surroundings. All this is perfectly normal. But at the end of a treatment you should be in a state of peace and deep relaxation.

The following 16 hand positions are a classic full-body treatment.

You can give yourself Reiki anywhere.

Head

Position 1. Face. Tips of fingers touching hairline. Hand position 1 covers the eyes, nose, sinuses, upper jaw, forehead and frontal lobes of the brain. It also regulates the pineal and pituitary glands, the thalamus and the hypothalamus. This position helps eye and sinus disorders, headaches, stress, strokes, colds and influenza.

Position 2. Sides of head. Fingertips touching on crown. Hand position 2 covers the right and left hemispheres of the brain and the glandular system. It helps to balance the hemispheres of the brain. It aids strokes, migraines, headaches, head injuries, motor and thinking functions and the nervous system.

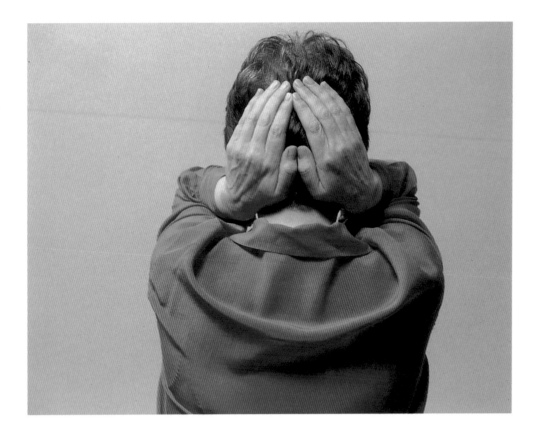

Position 3a. Back of head.
Thumbs touching. Hand position 3a covers the cerebral cortex and cerebellum, brain stem and glandular system. Again, it aids strokes, migraines, head injuries and the nervous system. It is also emotionally calming.

Position 3b. Alternative back of head.
Use whichever of these two positions feels comfortable at the time. Some practitioners feel that position 3a supports the balance and interaction of the hemispheres of the brain and that position 3b is better for the different functions of the cerebral cortex and cerebellum.

The above positions for the head improve the circulation to the brain, ease pressure on the skull and are deeply calming.

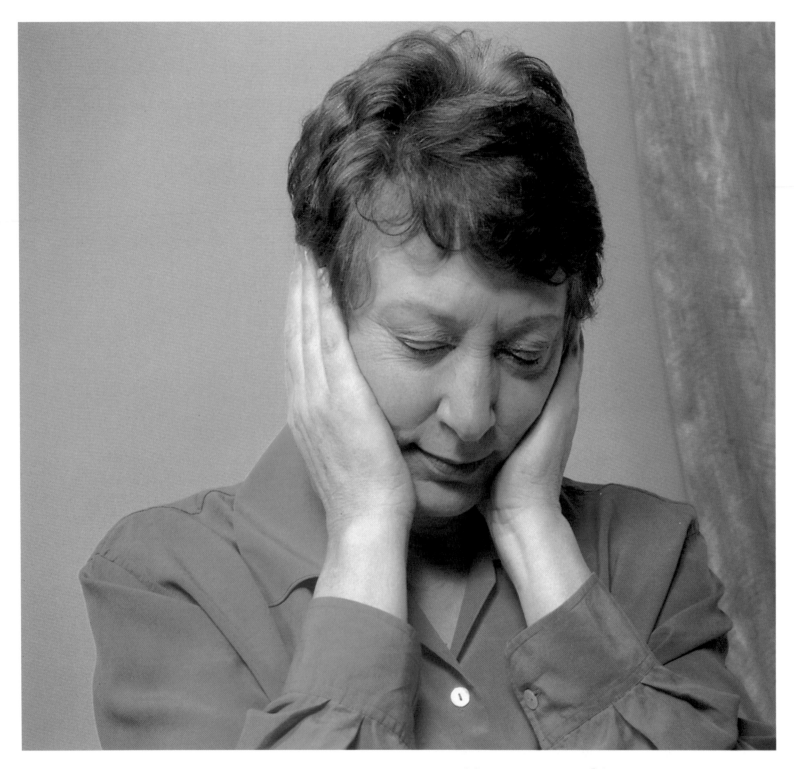

Position 4. Ears and jaw. Fingertips on ears. Position 4 covers the ears, Eustachian tubes, teeth, mouth and gums. It assists hearing and balance, ear, mouth and throat infections.

Front of torso

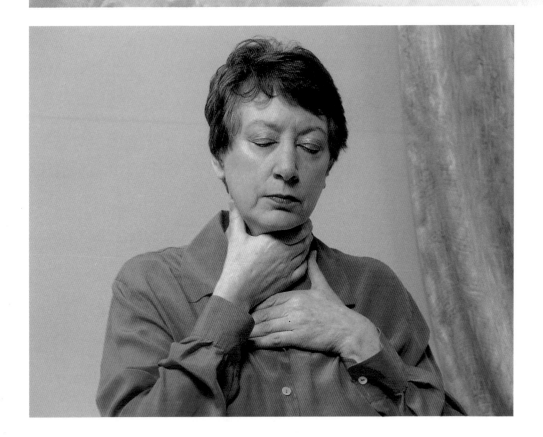

Position 5. Neck and thymus.
One hand on the neck, the other immediately below. Position 5 covers the throat, larynx, oesophagus, trachea and bronchi and the thyroid, parathyroid, thymus and lymph. It helps with throat problems, metabolism, weight, energy levels, calcium absorption, bronchitis, stress, nerves and the immune system.

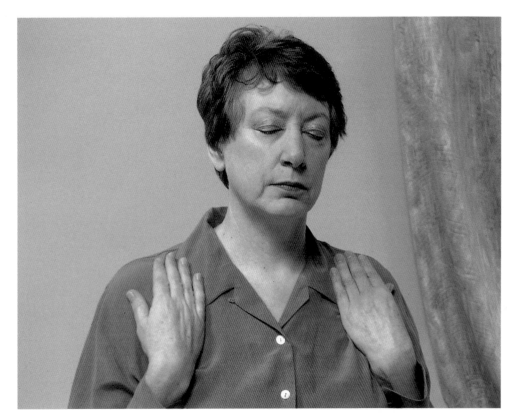

Position 6. Clavicles. Hands on collarbones. Position 6 covers the collarbones, ribs, shoulders and lung tips. It helps injuries, shoulder tension and breathing.

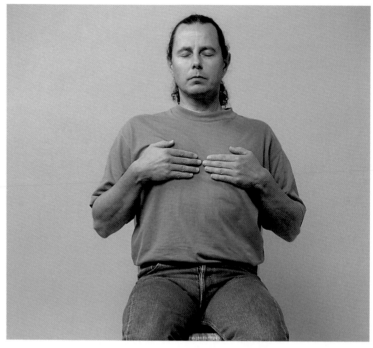

Position 7. Chest, breasts and heart. Female.
One hand on each breast or both hands cupping each breast.

Position 7a. Chest and heart. Male. One hand on either side of heart.

Position 7 covers the heart, lungs, ribs and lymph. It aids circulation, heart disease, breathing and lactation and helps to balance female hormonal production.

Position 7b. Heart. Some people, especially women, prefer to treat the heart separately. There is a tendency to put the hands in the middle of the chest, rather than towards the left, because the heart chakra is in the middle. This is the seat of love and it is very soothing.

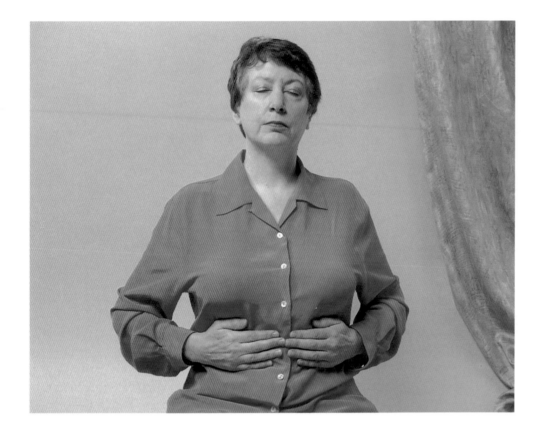

Position 8. Upper abdomen.
Position 8 covers the base of the lungs, the liver, spleen, stomach, pancreas, gall bladder, solar plexus, vagus nerve and major blood vessels. It helps to alleviate stress and shock, infections, diabetes and blood and gastric disorders. It also helps to clear toxins.

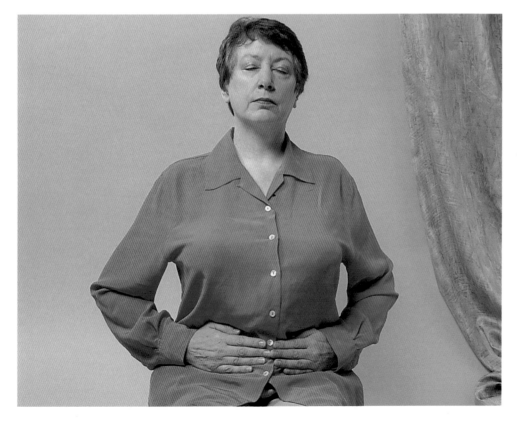

Position 9. Mid-abdomen.
Position 9 covers the intestines. It assists the absorption of nutrients and the digestion of food. It helps with candida, diverticulitis, colitis and other intestinal problems.

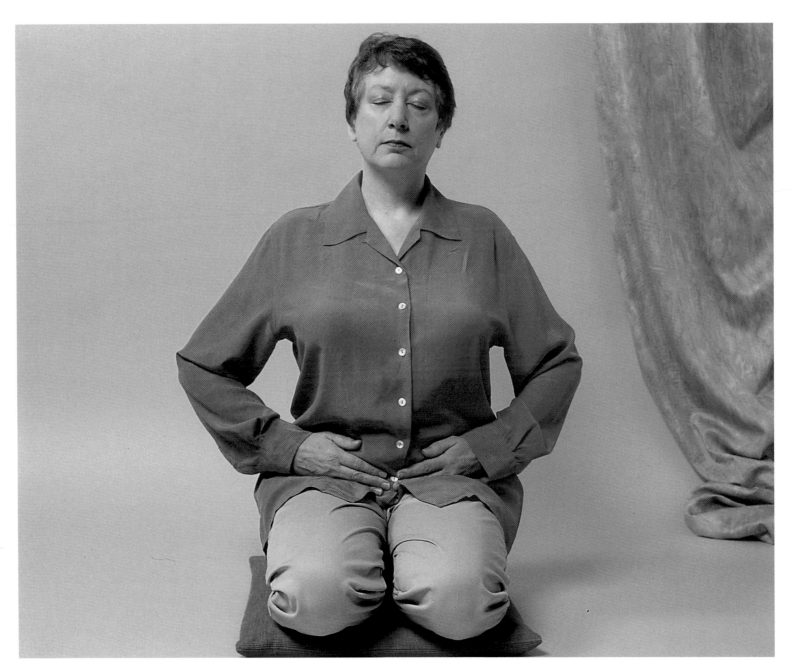

Position 10. Lower abdomen/genitalia.

Position 10 covers the lower intestines, bowel, bladder, uterus, ovaries, Fallopian tubes, vagina and prostate gland. It is helpful for intestinal, vaginal, urinary, menstrual and male and female sexual disorders.

If you have a urinary or genital disorder, you may wish to add an extra position by placing one hand on the pubic bone and the other over the penis or vagina.

Back of torso

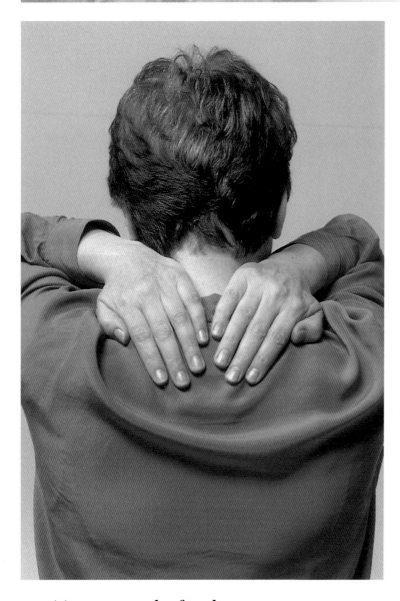

Position 11. Back of neck. Position 11 covers the nape of the neck and the spinal column. Fingers should be touching at the spine. It relieves neck and spinal stress and releases tension in the muscles of the shoulders and neck. It can be helpful in alleviating headaches.

Position 12. Shoulders: front view.
Position 12 shows that the elbows can be treated at the same time. It is also possible to cover the upper or lower arm instead of the elbow with the free hand.

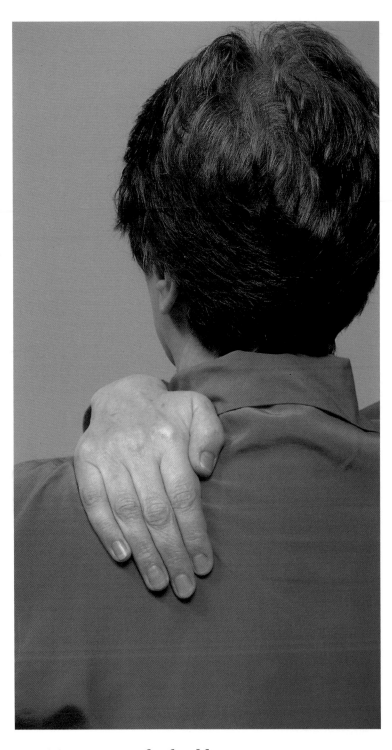

Position 12a. Left shoulder.

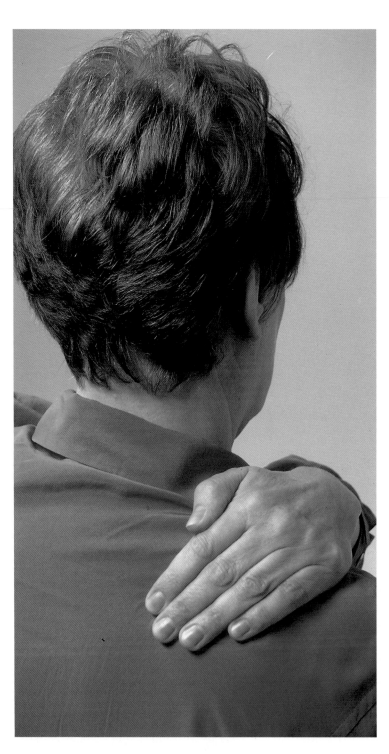

Position 12b. Right shoulder.

This covers the shoulders, scapula and the top of the ribs. It assists shoulder tension. It also covers the top of the lungs. Change hands to cover each shoulder.

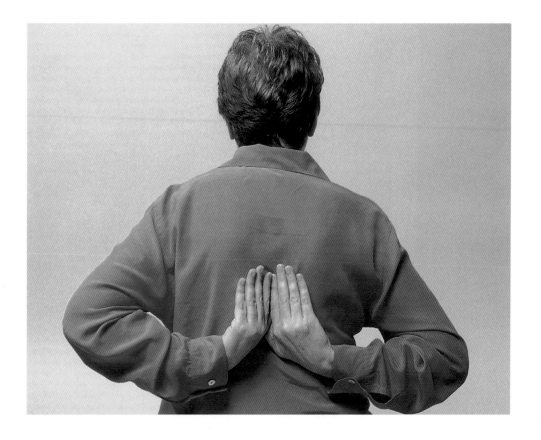

Position 13. Back of heart.
Position 13 covers the back of the heart, lungs, ribs and spinal column. It eases spinal tension, supports the action of the heart and aids breathing problems.

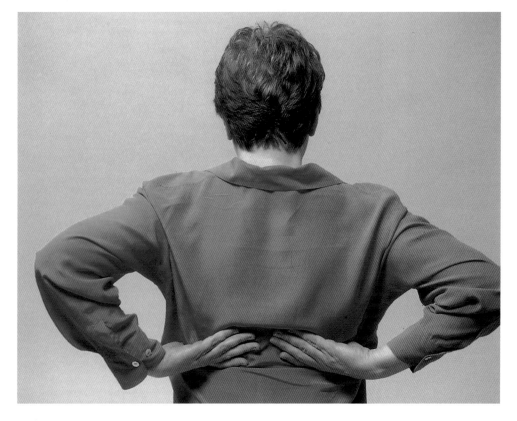

Position 13a. Alternative back of heart.
Position 13a emphasises the lungs and ribs. Choose whichever position feels more comfortable.

Position 14. Lower ribs. Position 14 covers the lower ribs, spine, the base of the lungs, the kidneys, adrenals and the back of the stomach, spleen, liver, gall bladder and pancreas. It helps to alleviate stress and shock, kidney, spinal, rib and lung problems. It also supports the bust position 8. The adrenal glands have many functions, so this position is helpful for ailments as diverse as arthritis and headaches.

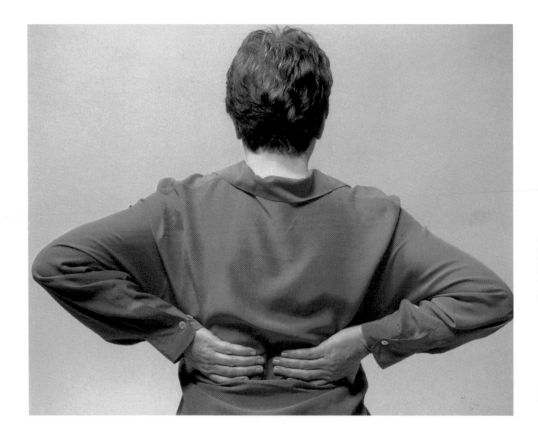

Position 15. Lumbar. Position 15 covers the lumbar region of the spine, pelvis, intestines, ureters and hips. It helps to alleviate stiffness of the lumbar region and sacroiliac joint. It helps hip and pelvic rotation. It also eases sciatica and intestinal problems.

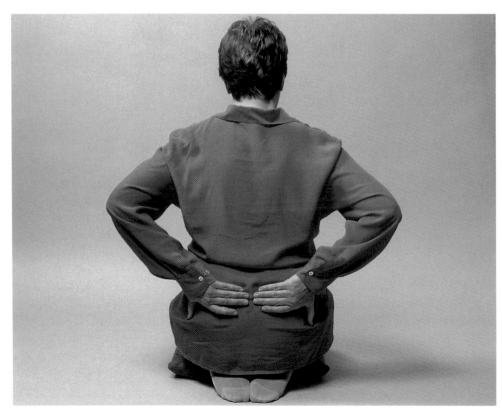

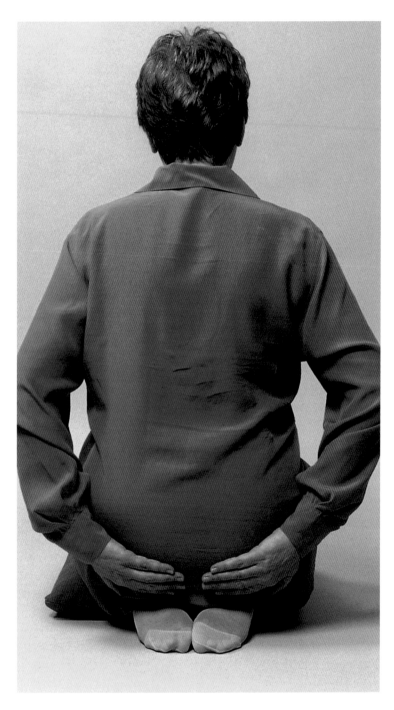 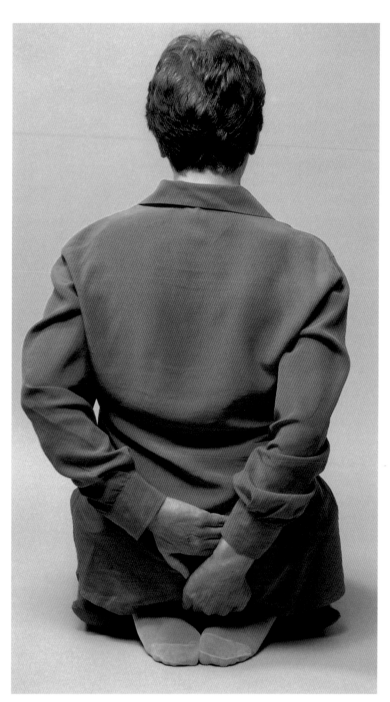

Position 16. Base of spine.

Position 16 covers the sciatic nerve, sacrum, coccyx, pelvis, hip, rectum and anus. It aids the relief of haemorrhoids, stiffness of the sacrum and coccyx, sciatica and hip and pelvic rotation. It also treats the reproductive and urinary areas from the back.

Position 16a. Base of spine.

An alternative position, which emphasises the sacrum and coccyx, rectum and anus. One hand is placed across the sacrum, the other is placed along the coccyx.

Hand positions (one on one)

Before very long, you will want to try out your new Reiki skills on your friends and family. What do they think about it? What can they feel? Has it healed them? Has it made them feel better? All these are common human concerns and the proper business of Level I. You need reassurance and feedback, little successes and triumphs.

Just a few months after I first learned Reiki, my older friend and I had a lovely surprise. She had had a nasty fall. Her shin was badly grazed and painful. I asked her if she would like some Reiki. I started to work on her leg. My hands kept going down to her feet. I was puzzled. Suddenly she became very excited. 'I can wiggle my toes!' she said. Her toes had been so stiff that for years she had been unable to move them. She was more excited about her feet than her leg. But her leg was less painful and did heal quickly.

When you are learning Reiki, you may assume that you have to try to give it. Nothing could be further from the truth. Reiki just happens. The more you try, the more you will block it.

Please let go and trust.

When you ask Reiki, your psyche or a spiritual source for help, just state your need and let Reiki do the rest. If you are worried, thoughts may be churning around in your head. Try to observe them and let go. Thoughts may arise that bring solutions to the problem.

When you put your hands on yourself or someone else to give Reiki, they will start to feel warm or may tingle, or both. Reiki will flow from your hands, usually for a minute or two before you feel that it is stopping or your hands have become cool. You will feel hesitant for a while until you get used to the sensations. Within a week or two, you will feel reasonably confident. The more you practise, the more obvious it will become.

If your master has a local sharing group or your classmates want to start one, you can practise your new-found skills in a safe environment. You can share your successes and concerns, ask questions and receive Reiki at the same time.

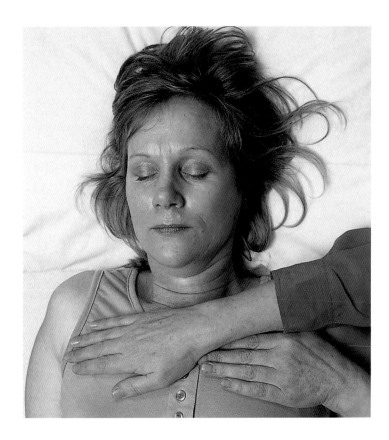

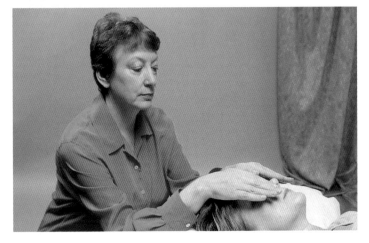

Whole-body treatments

One of the things that you need to understand is why you should give a whole-body treatment. Reiki attempts to heal the cause of the disease, as well as its symptoms. The cause may be physical in origin, such as bad diet, or it may be mental, such as stress. It may stem from an imbalance in another part of the body, such as whiplash, in which case the whole spine and skull should be treated.

Medical professionals have a term called 'referred pain'. It means that a pain in one part of the body may be connected to a problem in quite a different part. Thus a pain in the upper arm may be symptomatic of a heart problem. Headaches are notoriously difficult to pinpoint. A headache can be caused by stiffness of the neck, an infection, kidneys, menstruation or even bad feet, and these are only a few of the possible causes.

Reiki attempts to balance the whole energy system. For instance, the endocrine system is interactive. To treat just the adrenals for stress is only part of a treatment. The pituitary and hypothalamus play a major part in the proper functioning of the adrenals. Once you deal with these glands, the other glands can adjust to a better state of equilibrium. The whole body – bone, muscle, cartilage and so on – can relax and release tensions. Your mind can relax and your spirits can rise.

When you give Reiki, it pours into your crown chakra, down to your heart and out through your hands. Thus each time that you give Reiki you receive it first. As you can imagine, giving a treatment is normally a very pleasant experience.

Head

Position 1. Hands on face.

Heels of hands at the hairline. The face is very sensitive, so approach it gently. Avoid pressing the nose, restricting breathing or tickling.

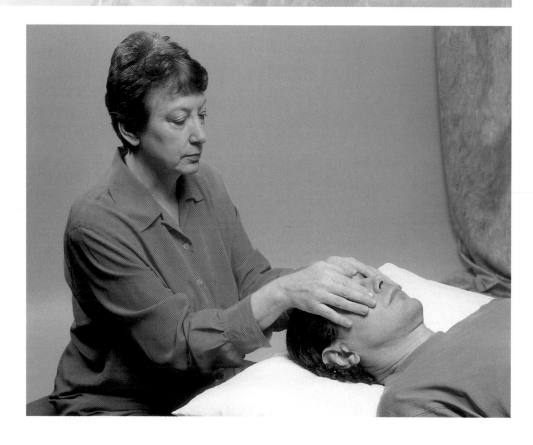

Position 1a. Hands off face.

Many people prefer to treat the face one or two inches off the body. This avoids any possible discomfort. However, do be careful not to touch or tickle accidentally.

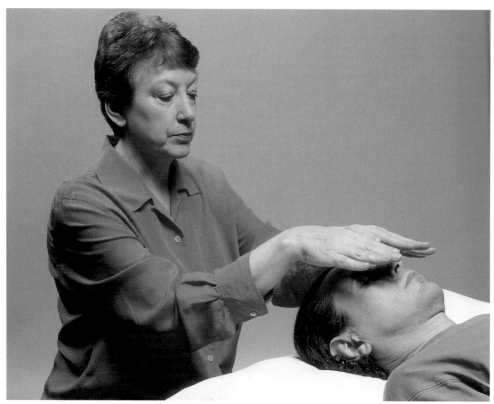

Position 2.
Sides and top of head.

Keep the heels of the hands together on top of the head.
Fingertips should be just above the ears.

Turning the head

The person being treated may already be deeply relaxed or even asleep. The following photographs show how to turn the head with the minimum disturbance. Avoid pulling the hair.

Right-handed method

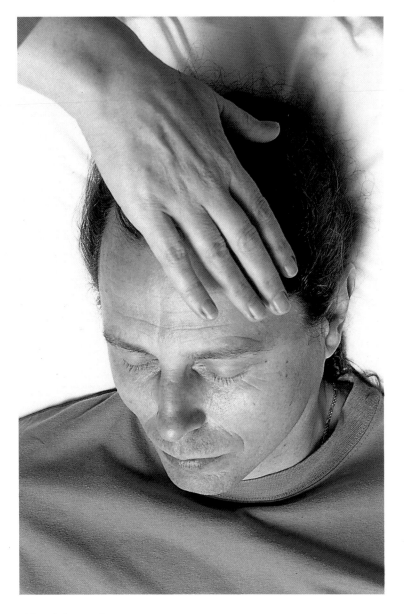

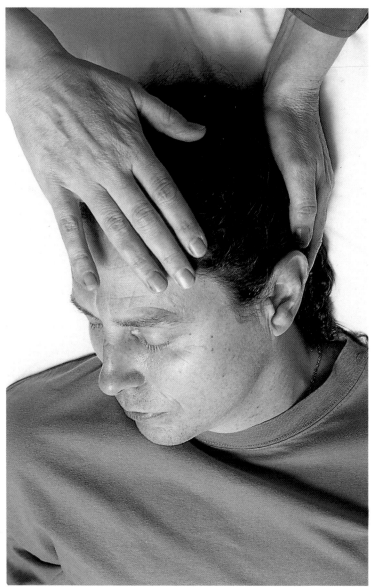

Position A.
Put your right hand to the subject's left temple and gently turn their head towards the right.

Position B.
Slip your left hand under their head.

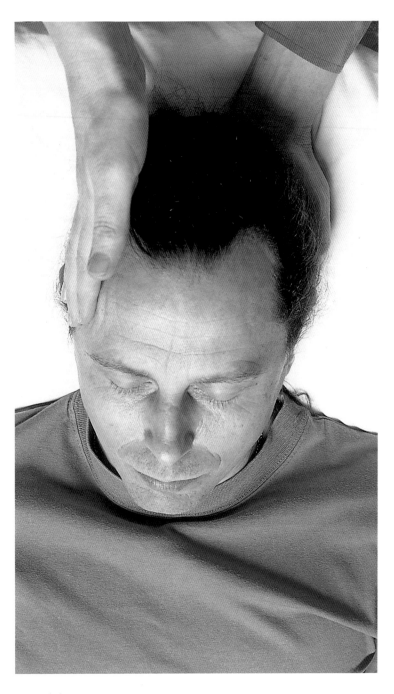

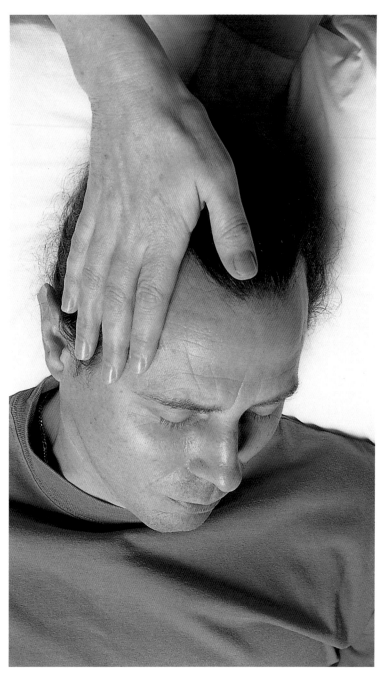

Position C.
Put your right hand to their right temple.

Position D.
Turn their head to the left.

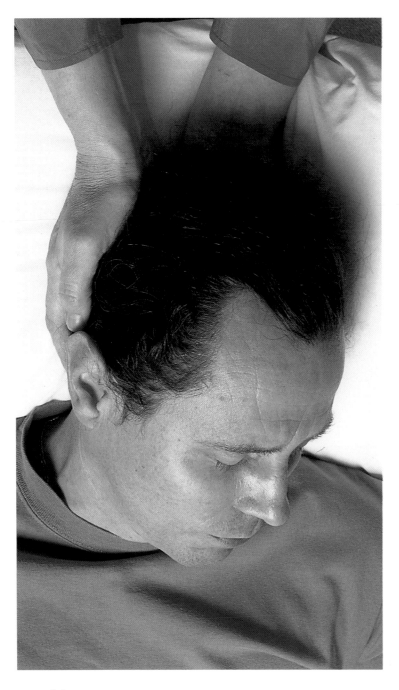

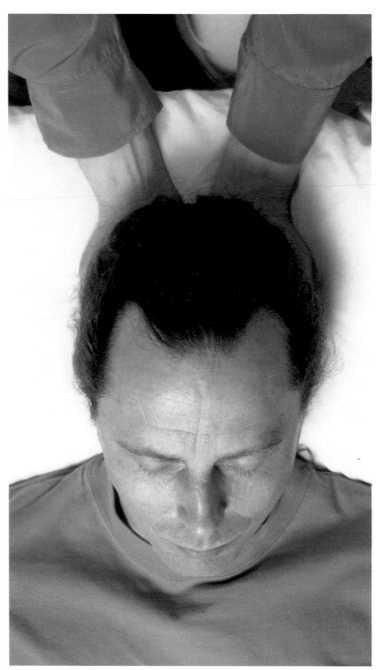

Position E.
Slip your right hand under their head.

Position F.
Allow their head to fall comfortably onto both of your hands.

Left-handed method

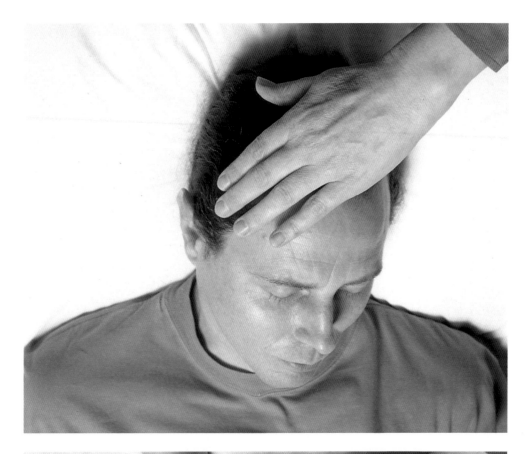

Being left-handed myself, I know how confusing it can be to follow right-handed instructions and to try to reverse them.

Position A.
Put your left hand to the person's right temple and gently turn their head to the left.

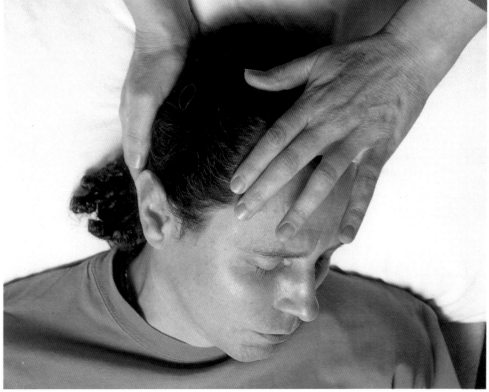

Position B.
Slip your right hand under their head.

Position C.

Put your left hand to their left temple.

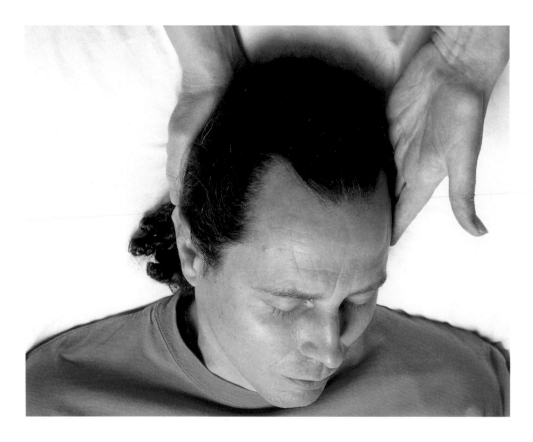

Position D.

Turn their head to the right.

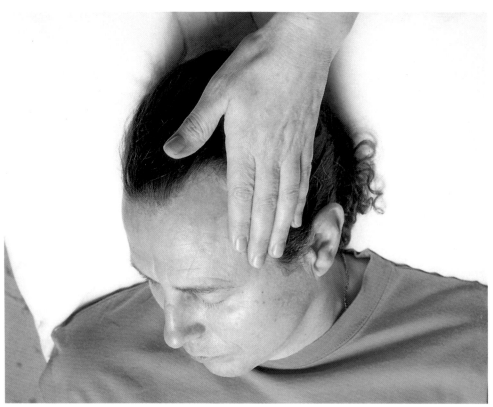

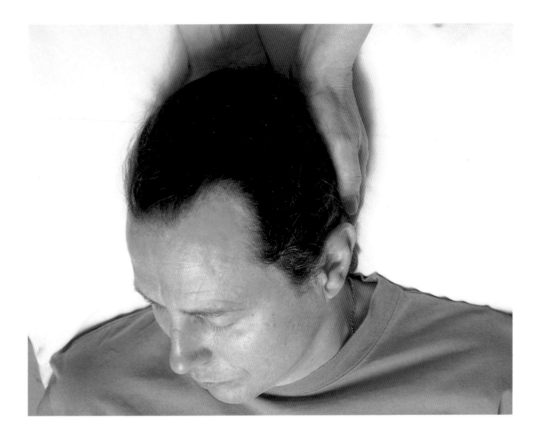

Position E.
Slip your left hand under their head.

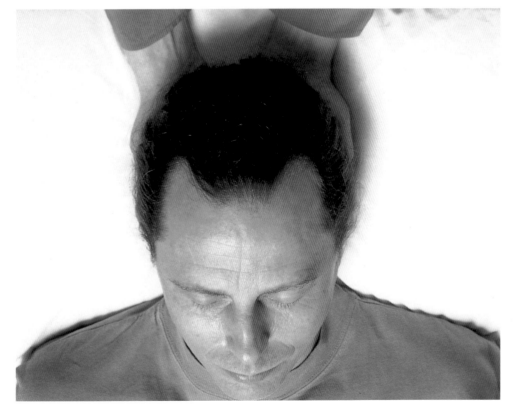

Position F.
Allow their head to fall comfortably onto both of your hands.

Front of torso

Position 3. Back of head.

The palms of the hands cradle the skull and the fingertips cover an inch or two of the neck. The hands should be touching each other.

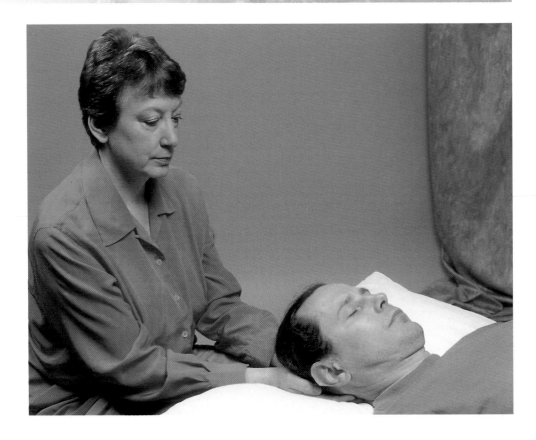

Position 4. Ears and jaw.

Slip your hands gently from behind the head onto the ears and jaw, being careful not to pull the hair or to jar the head with a sudden movement. The palms cover the ears and the middle fingers follow the jaw line.

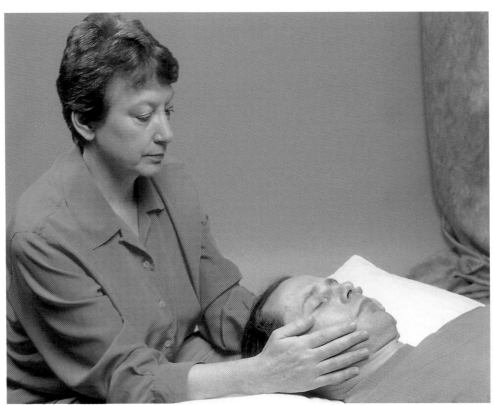

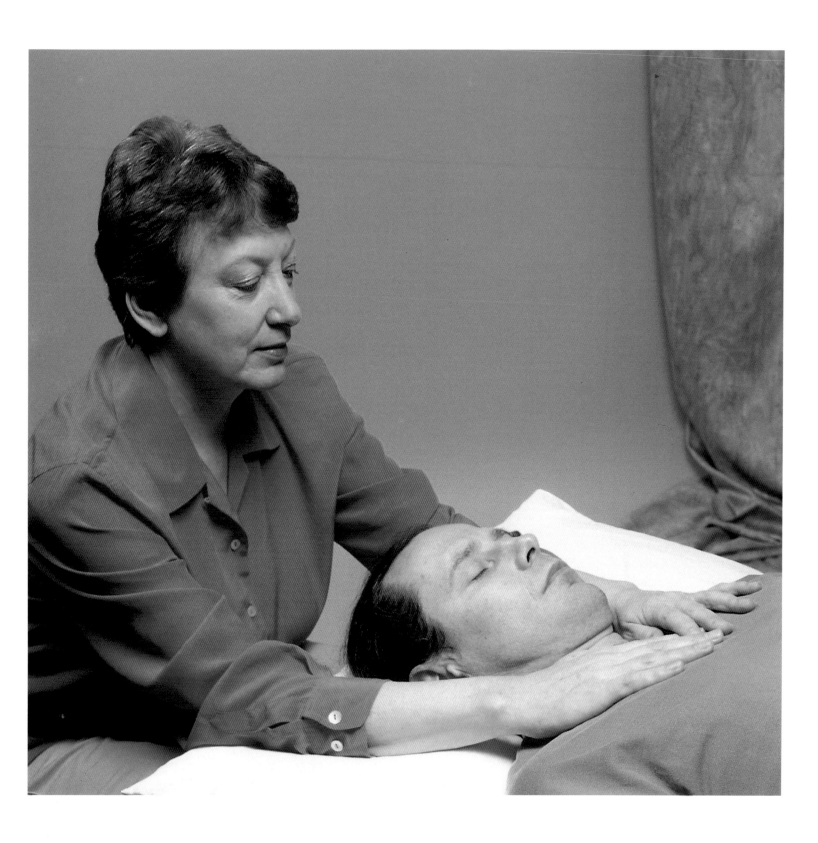

Approaching the neck and throat

The throat is a sensitive area. It is best that you treat another person from one or two inches off the body. Therefore the throat and neck positions have been split. Avoid touching the face with your arms and clothing in positions 5 and 6a.

Position 5a.
Gently turn the head.

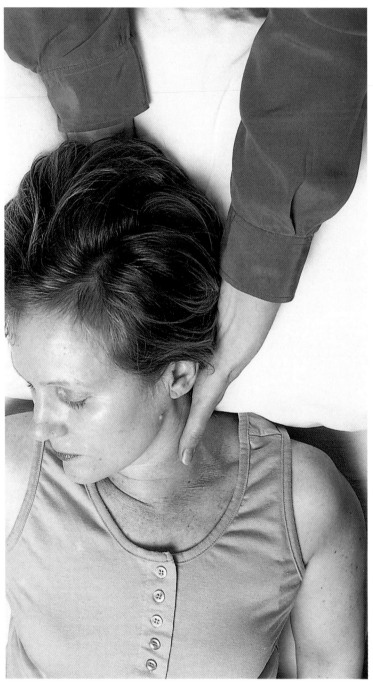

Position 5b.
Slip one hand under the neck.

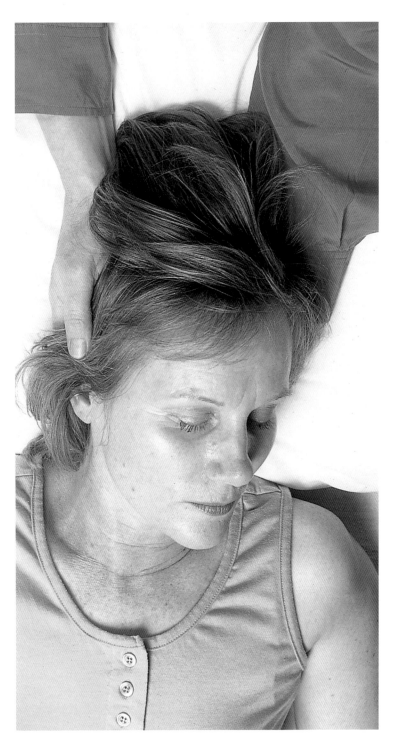

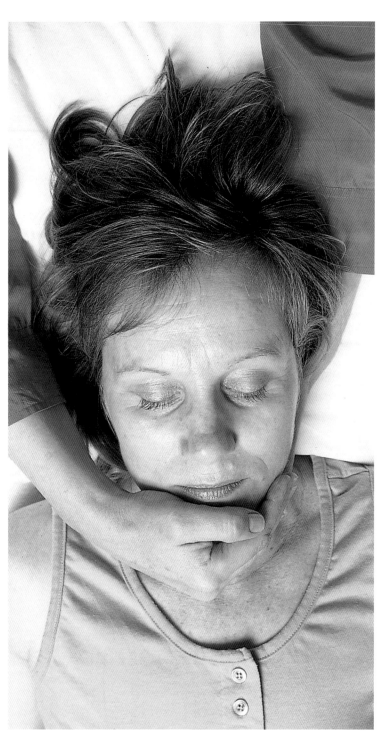

Position 5c.
Turn the head to the centre and remove your other hand.

Position 5d.
Cup your thumb and first finger over the chin. The remaining fingers are cupped above the throat.

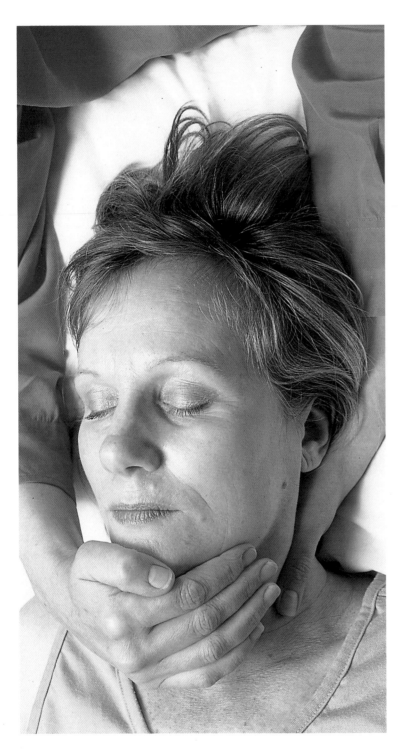

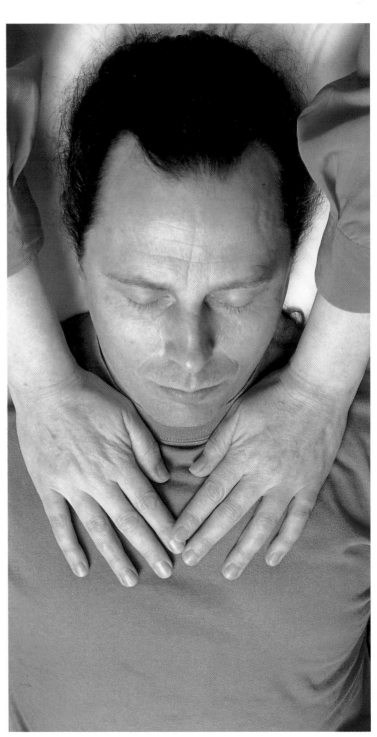

Position 5e.
Neck and throat. This shows the final position clearly from the side. You can rest your arms on the pillow.

Position 6.
Base of neck. The heels of your hands are resting on the neckline and your hands are touching.

Be careful not to trap any hair when using positions 5a to 5e.

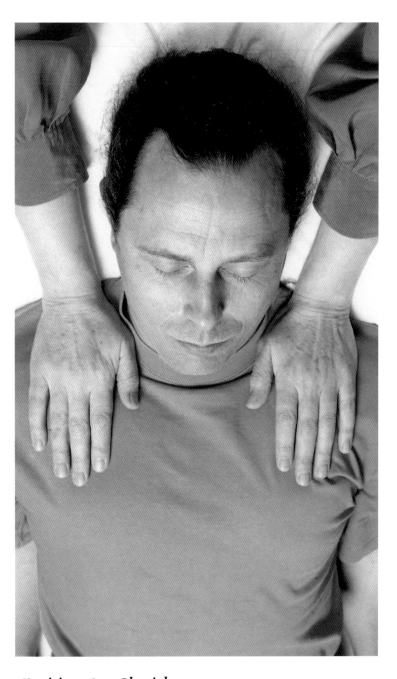

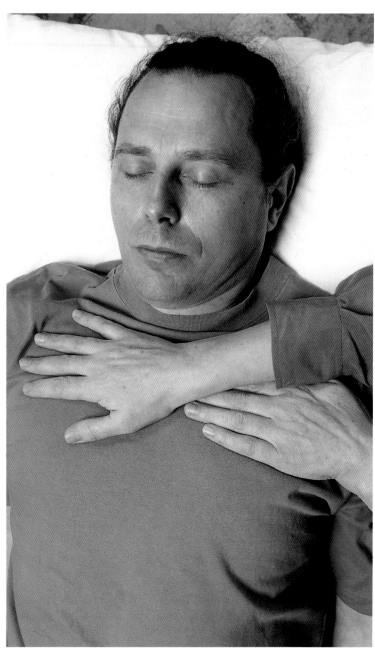

Position 6a. Clavicles.
Hands rest on the collarbones.

Position 6b. Alternative clavicles.
You can treat the clavicles and base of the throat from the side
of the body if you prefer.

In position 6b and the following front-of-body positions, check that your hands touch at the centre of the body.

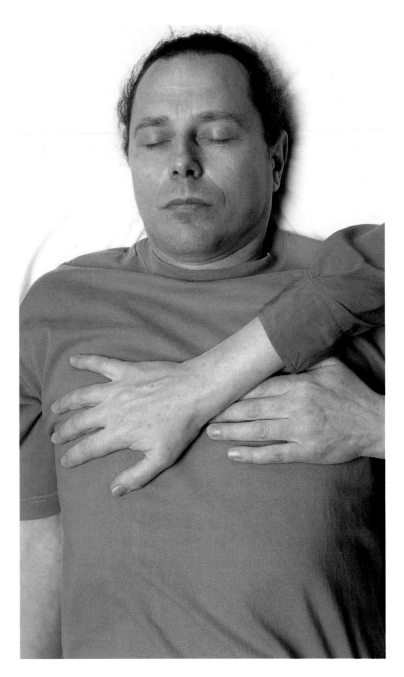

Position 6c. Thymus and upper chest.

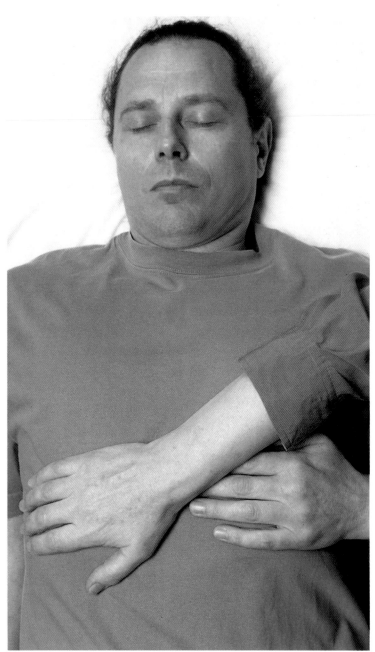

Position 7a. Heart and lungs. Male.

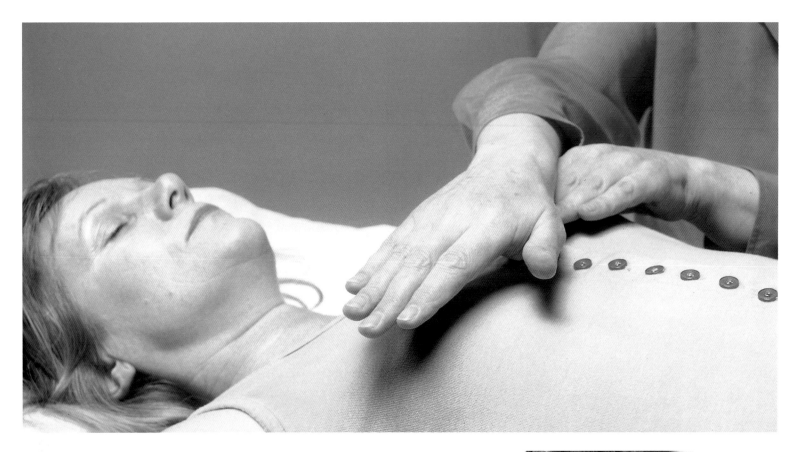

Position 7b.
Heart, lungs and breasts. Female.
Hold your hands an inch or two off the body.

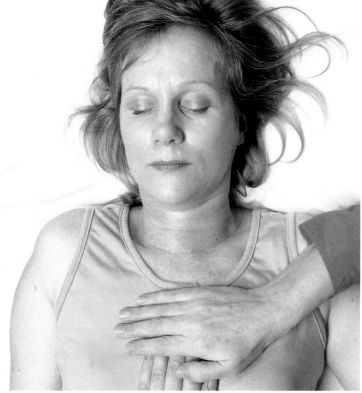

Position 7c. Heart.
Many people prefer to treat the heart separately, especially when treating females.

Position 8. Midriff.

Hands cover the base of the ribs and the stomach. For all hand positions that go across the body in this fashion, the hands need to touch. Here you can clearly see that the fingertips of the left hand touch the heel of the right hand.

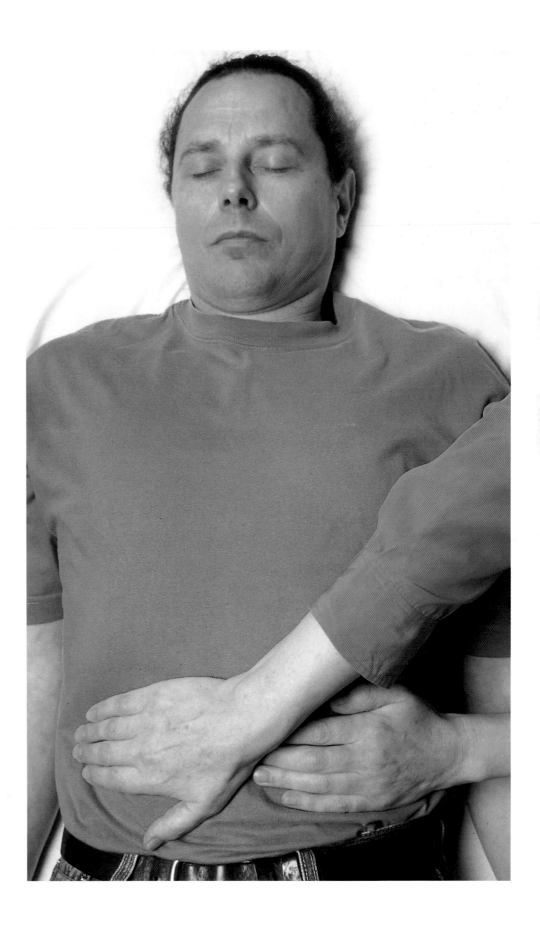

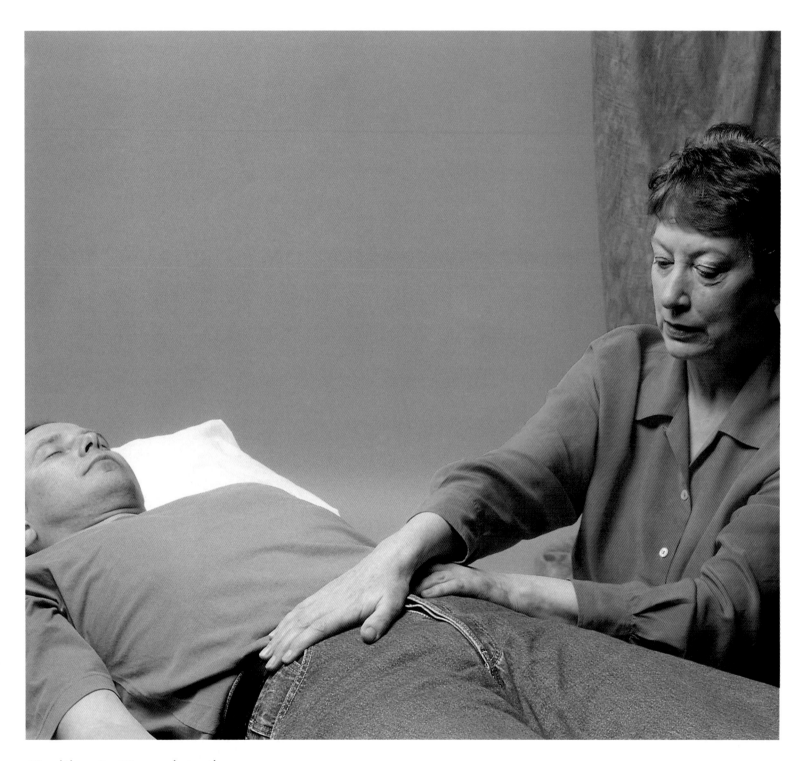

Position 9. Upper intestines.
Hands are immediately below the waist.

Position 10a.
Lower intestines, reproductive area. Female.
Hands are placed on the lower abdomen, just above the pubic bone.

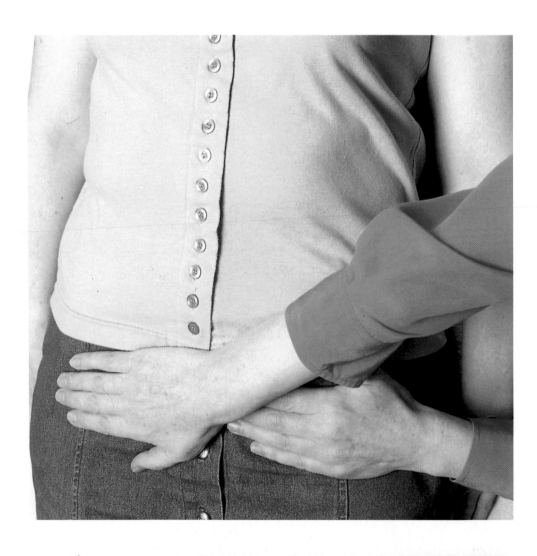

Position 10b.
Lower intestines, reproductive area. Male.
Hands are normally held an inch or two off the body when a male is being treated by a female.

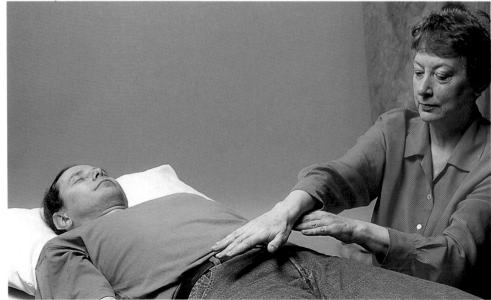

Back of torso

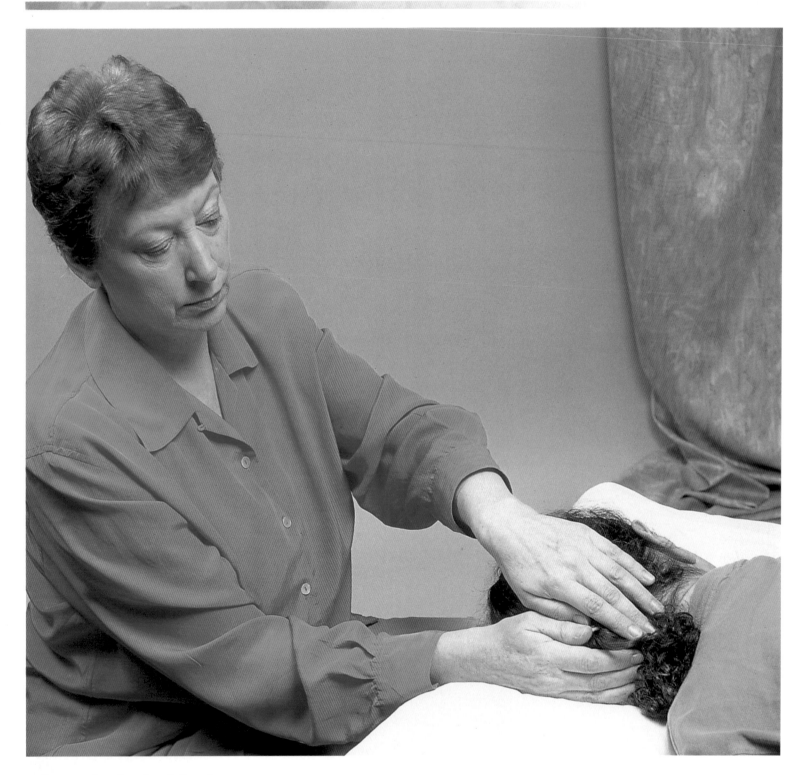

Alternative back of head.
Occasionally you may wish to treat the back of the head when the
person is lying face downwards. (Please refer to position 3, p55)

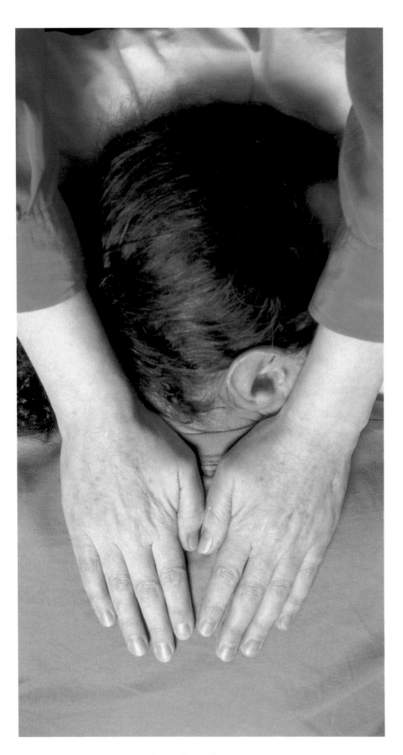

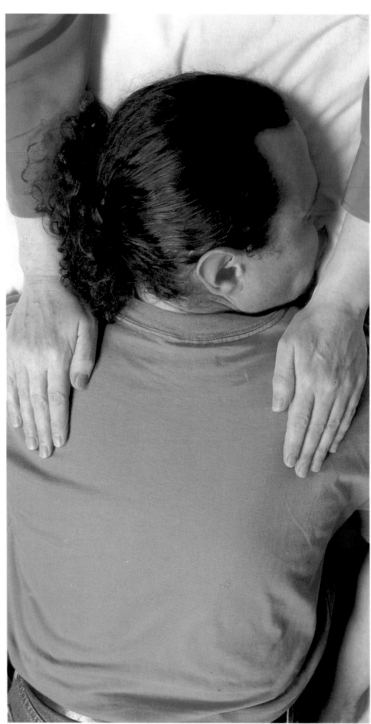

Position 11. Back of neck.
Both hands are on the nape of the neck, touching at the spine.

Position 12. Shoulders.
Hands are on the shoulder blades.

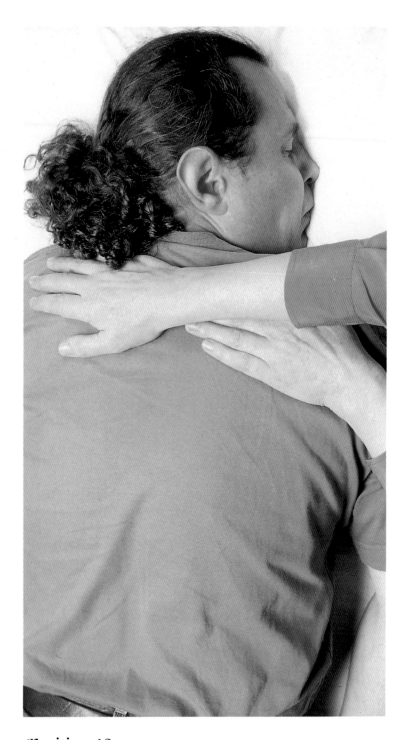

Position 12a.
Alternative nape of neck and shoulders.
This and position 13 can be done from the side of the body.

Position 13.
Back of heart, lungs and ribs.
Hands across the body, as in position 12a. Ensure that your hands touch in the middle.

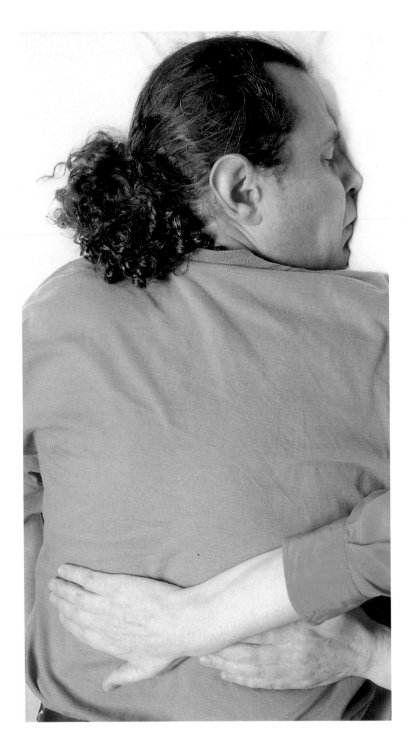

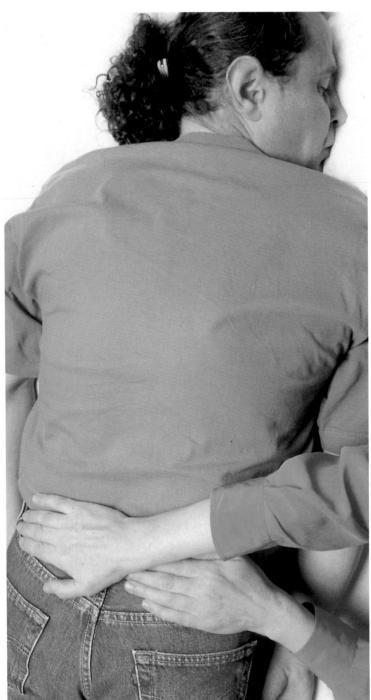

Position 14. Base of ribs.
Hands are immediately above the waist.

Position 15. Lumbar.
Hands are across the pelvis.

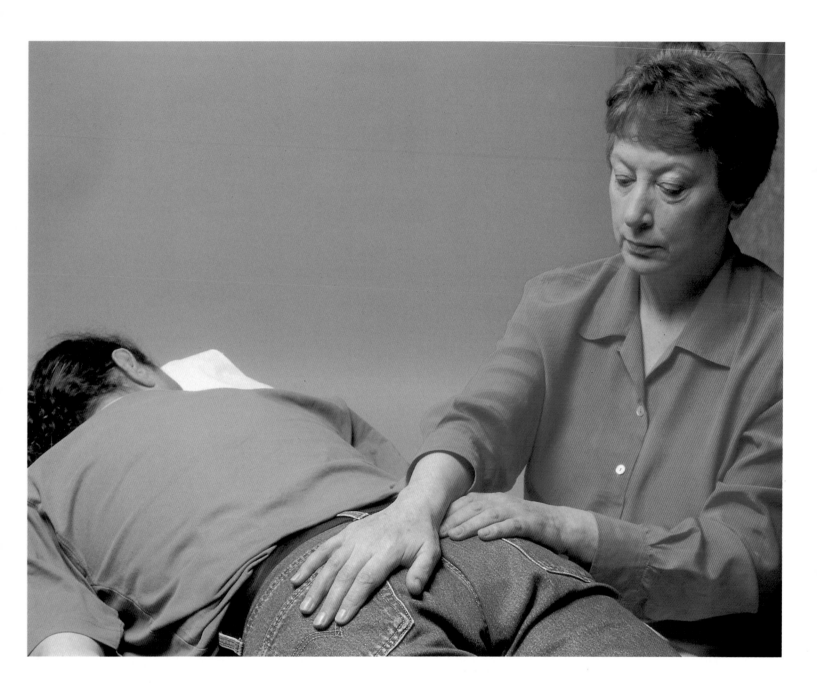

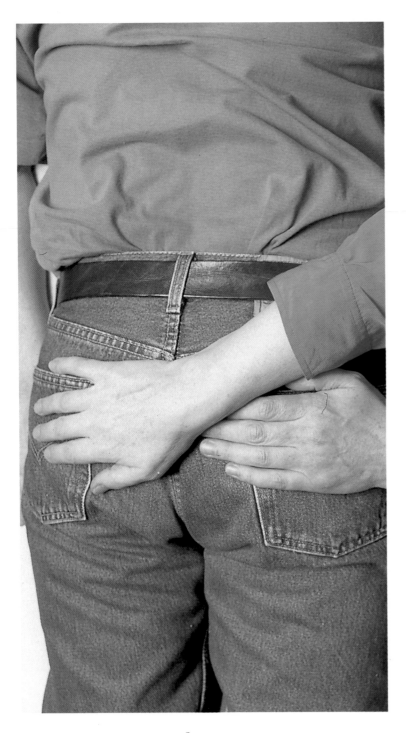

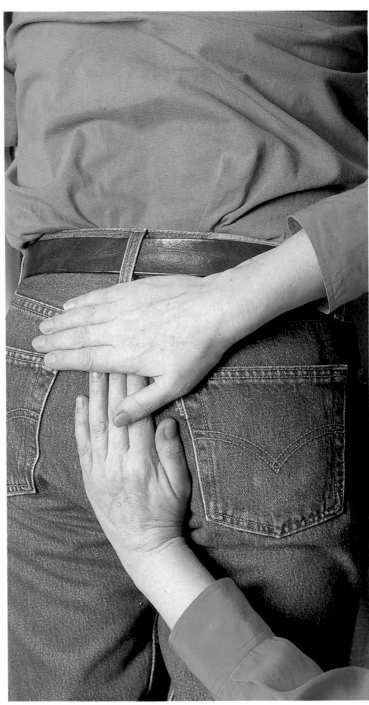

Position 16a. Buttocks.
Ensure that your hands meet in the middle, on the sacrum.

Position 16b. Sacrum and coccyx.
This alternative position emphasises the rectum and spine.

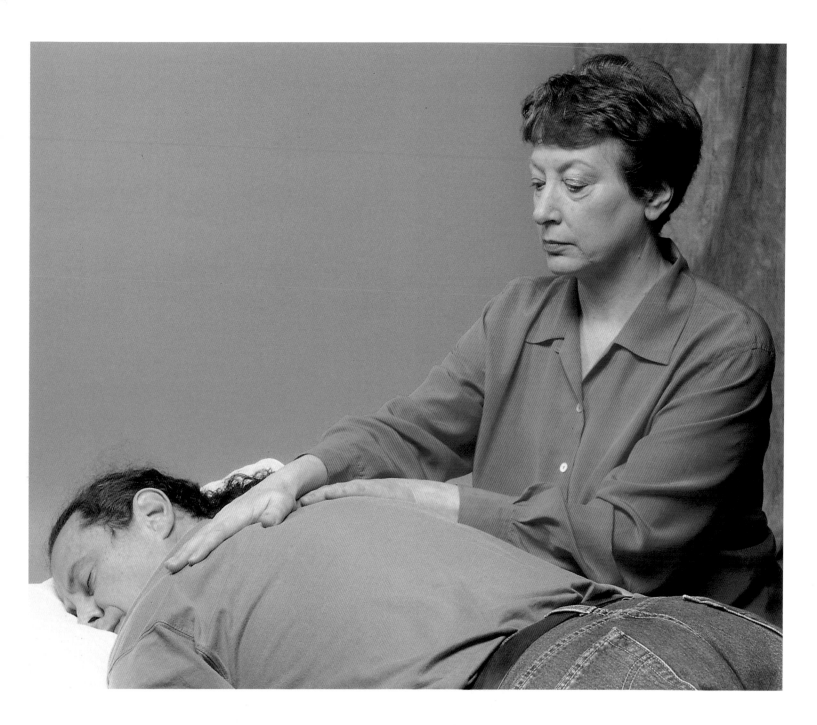

Please ensure that your hands meet in the middle of the body for positions 12a to 16a.
These positions cover the spine.

Group hand positions

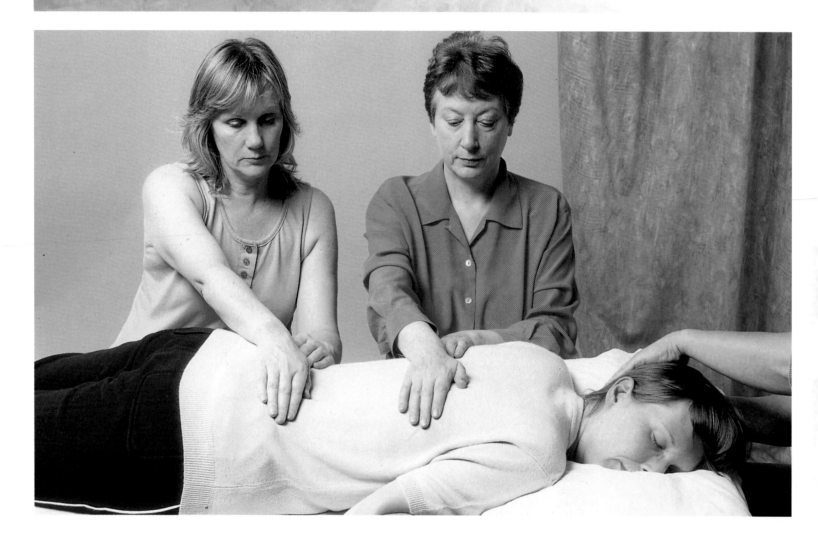

One of the most wonderful treats that Reiki has to offer is seven pairs of hands working on you simultaneously. There are many opportunities for this. One of the most common is a Reiki sharing group. Many masters host a sharing group. It is a very good way of experiencing Reiki for the first time and gives you a chance to ask lots of questions.

There are Reiki events from time to time around the country where Masters and students can meet, exchange Reiki and talk about their issues and discoveries. Your first taste of Reiki may be at a big exhibition where there is room for several people to work on you. Or your first taste of group Reiki may be your Level I class. Whichever it is, you are likely to find that you are unable to get off the table for a minute or two unless someone has done a grounding technique on you. Bliss!

A Reiki beginner needs lots of practice. Will it work? Are my hands warm? These are just two of the questions that inevitably arise for the learner. Group Reiki in the class and afterwards is a wonderful support while you are experiencing initial doubts, fears and triumphs.

Depending on the number of people in the group, the body is apportioned among the group, each person taking responsibility for one section. In a class situation, I make sure that everyone moves around the table and works on the different positions.

The following section shows two common ways of sharing out the body.

Front – hands abutting

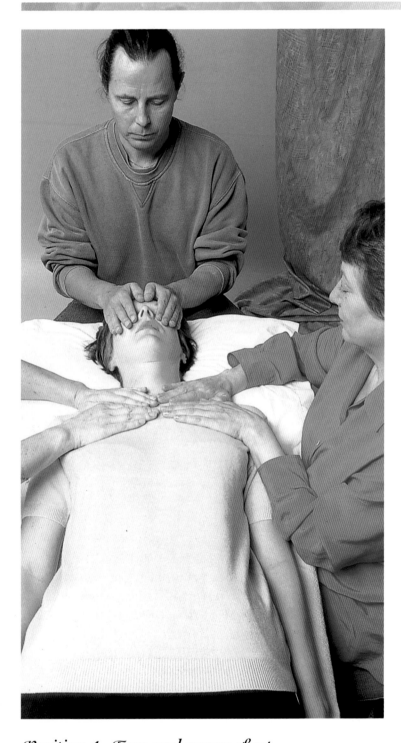

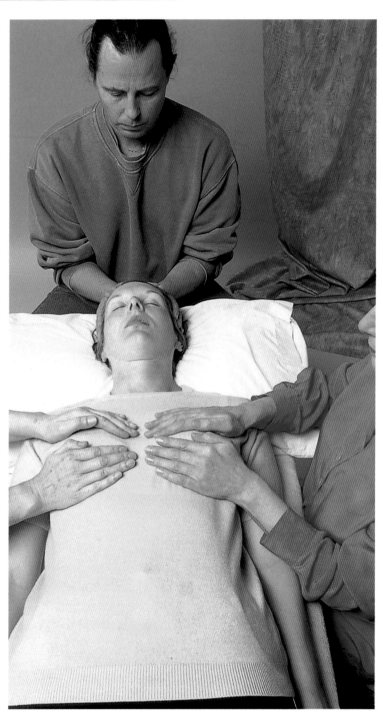

Position 1. Face and upper chest.
Two people sit opposite one another, with their hands touching on the sternum.

Position 2. Crown of head, chest, breasts.
This hand position touches the breasts, but not the nipples. This is usually comfortable in a group situation when the person being treated knows the people working on them.

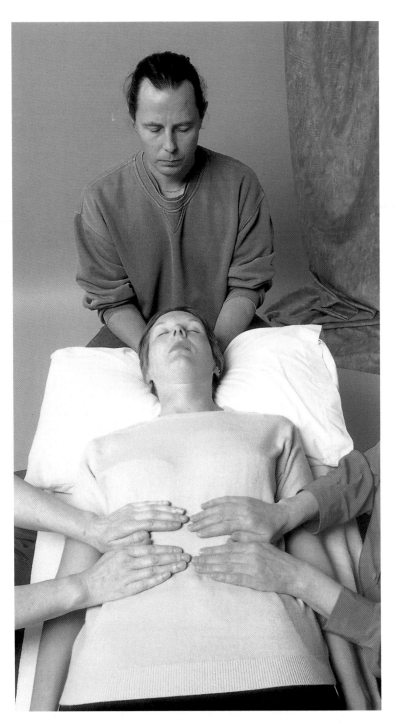

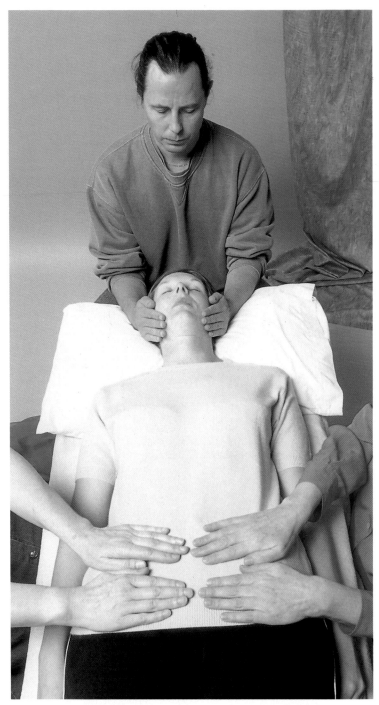

Position 3. Back of head, upper abdomen, lower ribs, stomach and waist.
Positions 1 to 4 comfortably cover the front of the torso.

Position 4. Ears and jaw, lower abdomen, intestines and genito-urinary functions.
In a group situation, it is perfectly in order to treat a male hands-on in this position.

Back – hands abutting

In this group, it has been decided that the person working on the head will work down to the back of the heart.

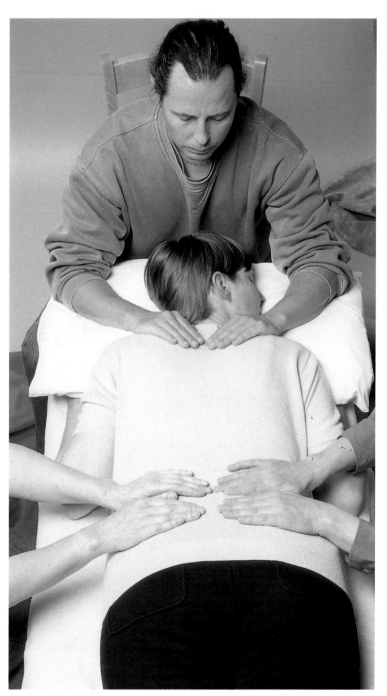

Position 5. Head, neck and lower ribs.
The two people sitting opposite one another work above the waist, their hands touching in the middle of the body.

Position 6. Nape of neck, waist and pelvis.
The person at the top of the table has moved on to the torso, whilst the other two work on the lumbar region.

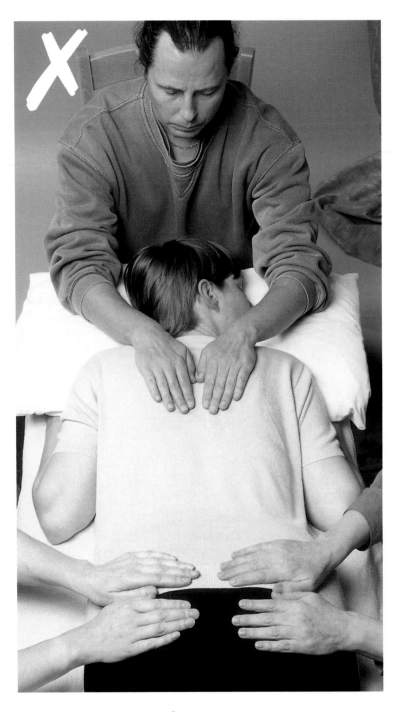

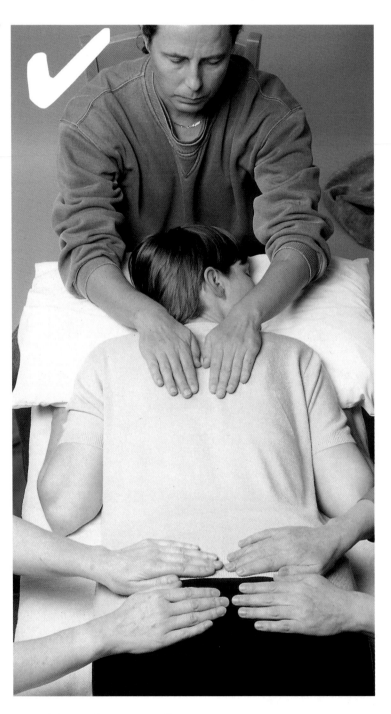

Position 7a. Buttocks:
Incorrect: the hands are not meeting at the spine.

Position 7b. Buttocks:
Correct.

It is important to check that you are covering the spine.

Front – hands offset

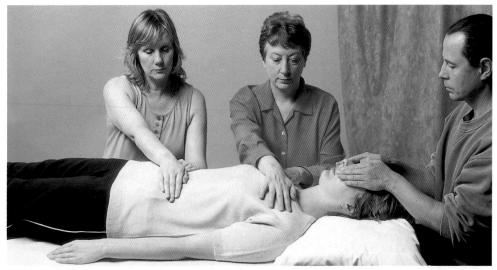

This group has decided that the person at the head of the table will work only on the head. The middle person is working on the upper torso and the third person is treating from the waist to the lower abdomen.

Position 1.
Face, upper chest and waist.
The two people treating the torso work with their hands across the body. Each has their hands touching in the centre of the body.

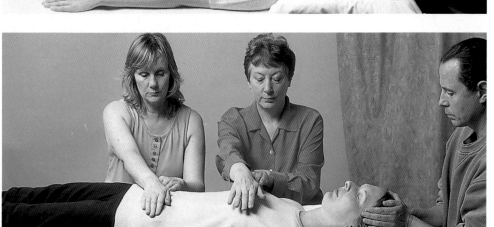

Position 2.
Sides and top of head, chest/breasts and upper intestines.
Hands should be held one or two inches off the breasts, unless you know one another well.

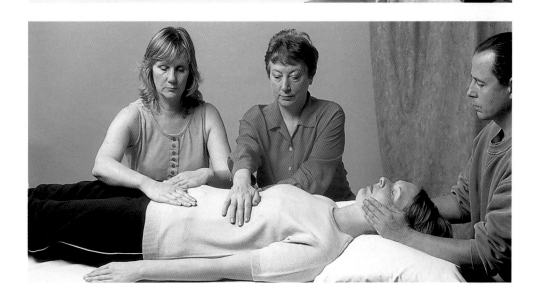

Position 3.
Ears and jaw, midriff and lower intestines/reproductive area.
In group Reiki there are often people who have learned with different masters and may have slightly different hand positions. The person treating the lower intestines has her hands in a 'V' position.

Back – hands offset

The group has decided that the person at the top of the table will treat down to the shoulders. The person in the middle is treating from the heart to the waist and the third person is treating below the waist.

Position 4.
Neck, heart and lumbar.
Notice that both hands are on the neck, which may be comfortably covered from this position.

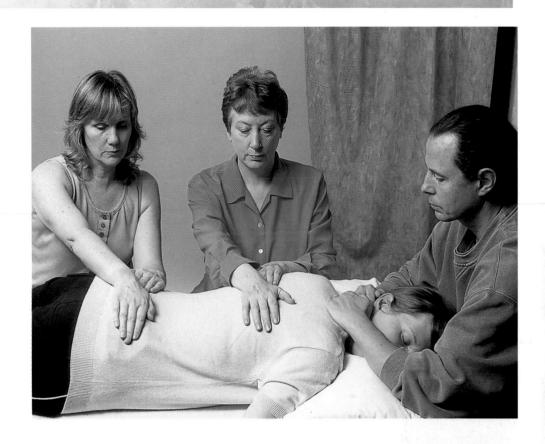

Position 5.
Nape of neck, lower ribs and buttocks.
Although some masters teach their students to treat to a regulated time (for instance, two minutes to each position), generally people move their hands when their hands cool off. If one person completes all of their moves before the others, they will often have to move to an extra position. The person working on the head may treat the outer shoulder. The middle person may treat the lungs and heart from the side or put in an extra position from the base of the ribs to the waist if the body is long from neck to waist. The third person may treat the hip joints from the side.

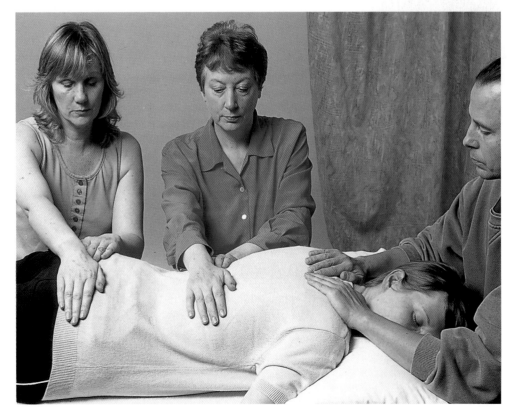

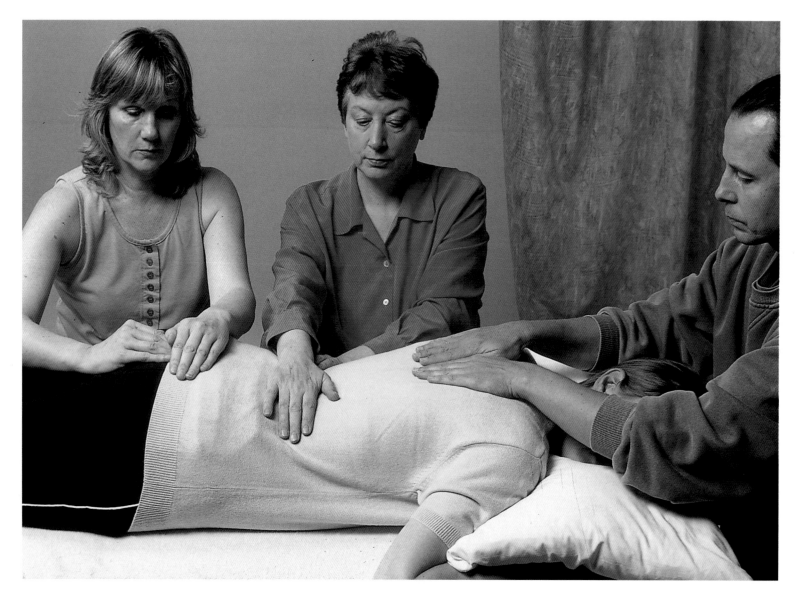

Position 6.
Shoulders, waist, sacrum and coccyx.

The person working on the lower torso is using the 'T' position:
one hand across the sacrum, the other straight up the spine over
the coccyx.

Treatments

The normal reaction to a Reiki treatment is one of profound relaxation. The client is placed fully clothed on a treatment couch. The session usually lasts from one to one-and-a-half hours. Short treatments can be given for specific ailments, such as sports injuries, on request.

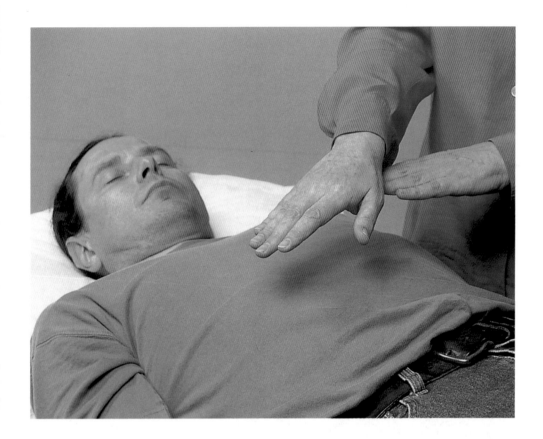

Your recipient may have asked for a treatment for a specific problem. Hawayo Takata always asked her clients what they wished to heal. She then commanded Reiki to heal it. This is a very Japanese attitude.

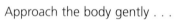

Approach the body gently . . .

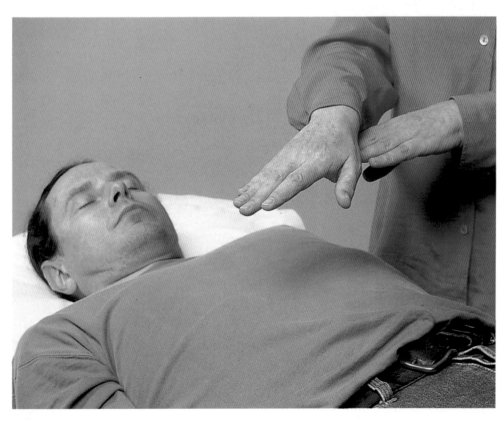

. . . and slowly.

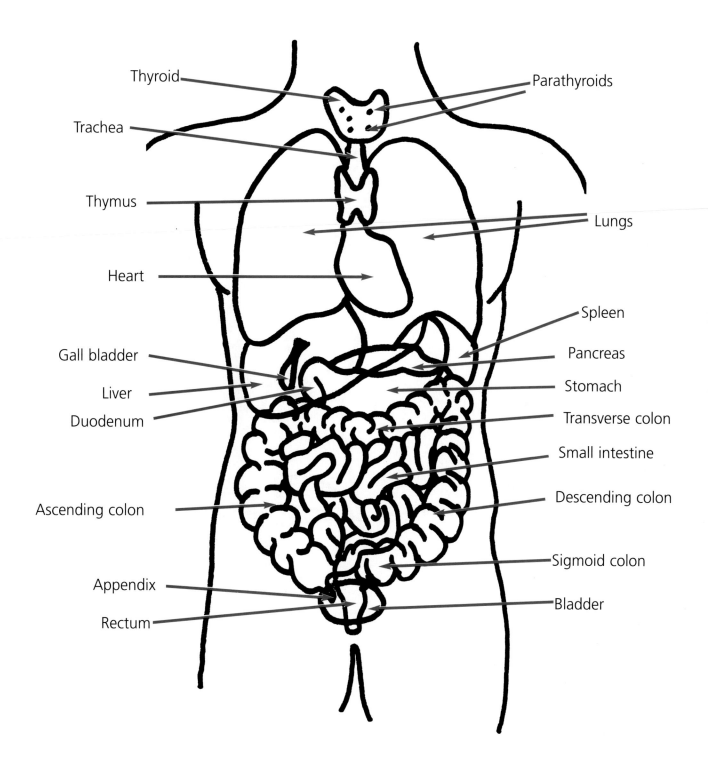

Thyroid

Parathyroids

Trachea

Thymus

Lungs

Heart

Spleen

Pancreas

Gall bladder

Liver

Stomach

Duodenum

Transverse colon

Small intestine

Ascending colon

Descending colon

Sigmoid colon

Appendix

Bladder

Rectum

The organs and glands of the body - front view

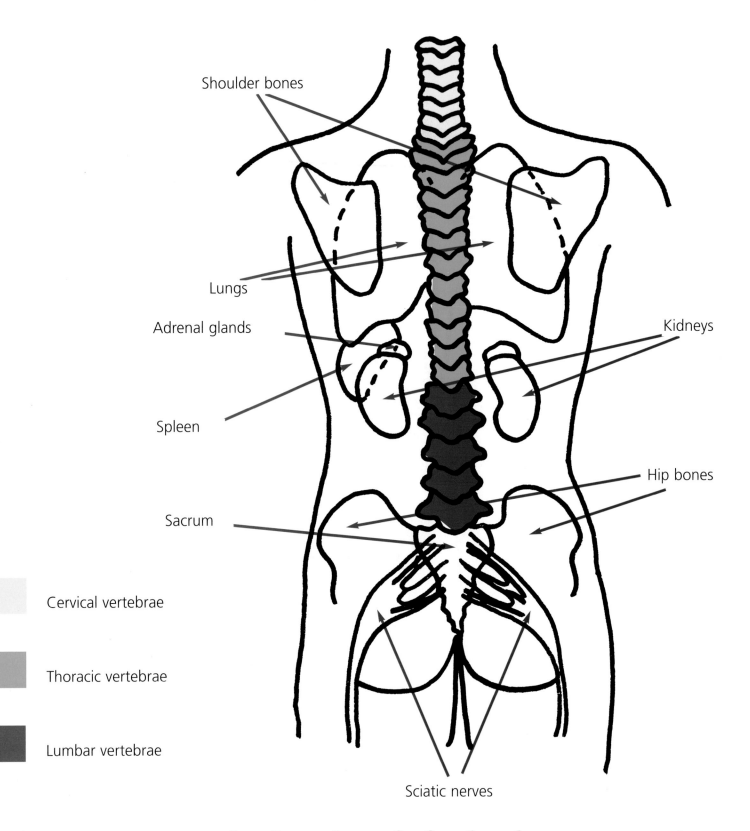

Shoulder bones

Lungs

Adrenal glands

Spleen

Sacrum

Kidneys

Hip bones

Sciatic nerves

Cervical vertebrae

Thoracic vertebrae

Lumbar vertebrae

The organs and glands of the body - rear view

The hands are gently placed on the body in a sequence of positions. Each position is held for a few minutes. If an area of the body is uncomfortable, the hands may be held off the body. As each hand rests on your body, you can feel heat or tingling coming from it. It is very soothing and relaxing.

Reiki tries to heal the cause of the disease, not just the symptoms. Therefore, although you may be delighted that your symptoms have disappeared after the first few sessions, you need to guard against disappointment in case there does not seem to be any instant cure. Sometimes, especially with chronic complaints, it may take a while to recover.

If you suspect that someone needs medical attention, you must say so. Sometimes the very fact that the Reiki practitioner is so adamant will help the subject face how ill he or she is. You are perfectly entitled to refuse to treat someone until they have visited a doctor.

Sometimes people find that although the original complaint may not have fully healed, there are other unexpected benefits. Another problem may resolve itself; the person may feel calm and unruffled for a few days afterwards. There are so many variables that it is impossible to predict.

Classes

When you learn Reiki, you will practise working on the different hand positions. You find that you can begin to feel heat when Reiki is flowing, and cooling when the energy has stopped flowing. You will quickly notice that your hands seem glued to certain positions, and you are unable to take them off. It is unnerving at first. It simply means that Reiki is still flowing into that area and that you need to wait until it has finished. You also have the chance to receive Reiki and to feel the warmth of the hands and to notice them cooling off. The master and students will ask for your feedback.

You will find that bodies are different. Some people take lots of Reiki, others relatively little. Some will take a lot of energy in a particular part of the body. Also, body shapes are different. Some people are long from neck to waist, others from waist to crotch, and in such cases you may need to add an extra hand position. If you have a big man on the couch, you may need to add two extra positions.

My classes usually begin with a meditation during which the Reiki energy pours into the students. It usually leaves them feeling calm and relaxed and ready to receive. Thereafter, each session may begin with either a meditation or a Reiki circle.

Reiki circles can be performed sitting or standing. The most usual kind is where everyone joins hands. You can also put your hands on each other's shoulders. People often like to have a Reiki circle before starting group healing in a sharing group.

Classes differ. Some are full of happy chat, others are quieter. When you are working on one another, you may be tempted to chatter on, but it is best to check that others do not find this annoying.

Grounding

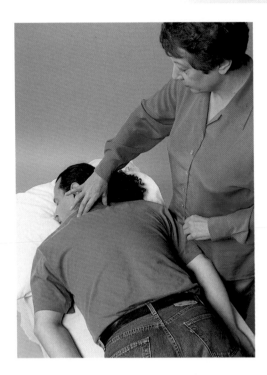

Position 1. Place your thumb and forefinger on either side of the spine, above the nape of the neck.

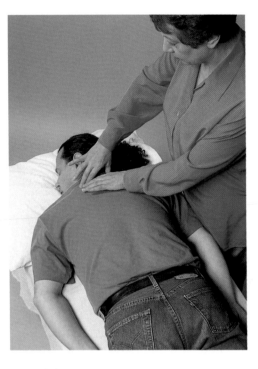

Position 2. Place the thumb and forefinger of your other hand immediately below.

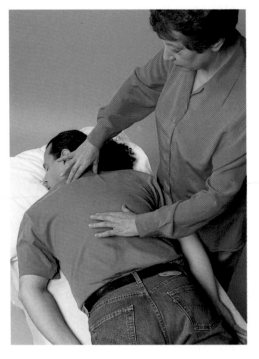

Position 3. Bring your hand swiftly down the body . . .

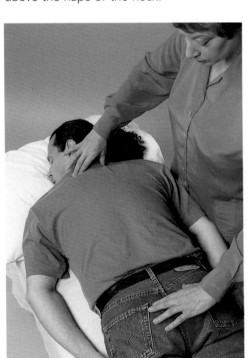

Position 4. . . . to the tail bone . . .

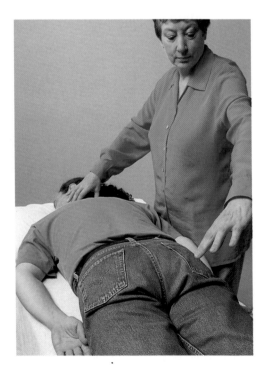

Position 4. . . . and off the body. Repeat steps 2 to 5 three times.

After a Reiki treatment, the person is often so deeply relaxed that it may take a minute or two before they are physically able to move. Sometimes you can leave them to indulge themselves for a while or you may need to move them quickly. Either way, it is important to ground your recipient if they are about to leave and drive a car.

The grounding sequence shown here is the best one that I know. It is a matter of preference. Your practitioner or master may give you a different method.

Depression

With depression, a person's needs have been unmet, or their life is so hard that they have become severely disheartened. The heart may be broken. Depression and other mental illnesses need a full-body treatment, but there will probably be more emphasis on the head. It is best treated with Level II techniques. In acute (or short-term) cases, the reason may be quickly seen and dealt with. Chronic depression may take some time.

Pregnancy and childbirth

Apart from the joy of giving Reiki to the unborn child, it helps to balance the hormones during pregnancy through to lactation, thus minimising morning sickness, emotional upset and post-natal depression. It is helpful for back pain, and many women have been delighted at its comforting warmth and the relief from pain during childbirth.

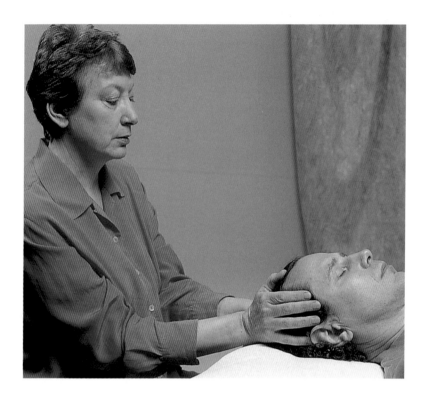

Treating children

Obviously, you will need to adapt the hand positions to the size of the child. A newborn baby will be covered in one position just by being held in your arms. I have seen the most remarkable changes in children. They normally respond very quickly to Reiki, and it is a pleasure for a parent to be able to comfort a sick or distressed child with Reiki.

Treating the very sick

From time to time you will need to give treatments to the bed-bound. Simply adapt the hand positions to the space available. There is no need to touch the body if it will disturb or distress the person. Sometimes a child or a very sick adult will become upset if they feel that people are too close. It is perfectly in order for you to hold your hands several inches off the body. Indeed, if you have done Level II Reiki, it might be better to give a distant healing, either at the bedside or wherever and whenever you feel the need.

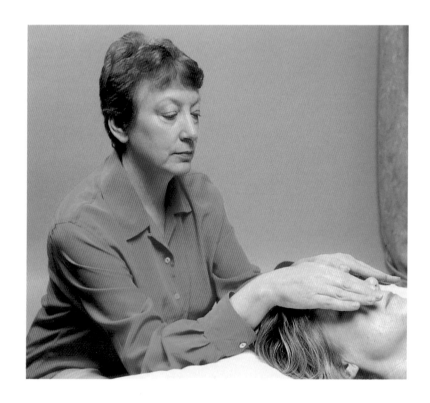

You do not have to treat someone's back. If someone is too ill to move, or movement is painful, Reiki will simply direct whatever is needed through the body to the back. When someone you love is very sick, there is a temptation to try too hard in an attempt to heal him or her. You cannot over-give Reiki. If you try, you will feel very uncomfortable.

Other methods of full-body treatment

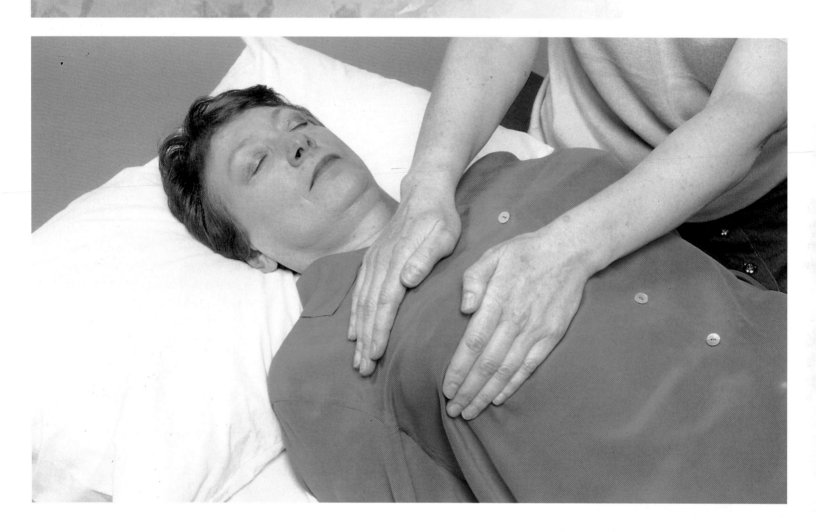

An alternative full-body treatment

For many years, Westerners were intrigued as to what Dr Usui taught and the way in which he taught it. We had only Hawayo Takata's information from Dr Hayashi. We were not sure when Dr Usui lived, how many students he had, and how many masters he created. Finally, in the last few years of the 20th century, we discovered students and masters of disciples of Dr Usui who were able to tell us about the Reiki Society that Dr Usui had founded. Documents with Dr Usui's seal were discovered, and, quite independently, copies of his teaching manual were found. Some Japanese masters agreed to come to the West and teach Reiki the way that they had been taught. What has emerged is a remarkably consistent picture of Dr Usui's teaching.

According to some sources, Reiki was originally taught in six degrees, and Dr Usui would give the initiation after the person had achieved the necessary skills. Hawayo Takata presented us with three degrees. She seems to have developed her teaching and practice during the 44 years from 1936 to her death in 1980.

Hawayo Takata was reported to have said that Dr Hayashi formulated the full-body treatment that she originally taught. It started with the *hara,* the Japanese word for the abdomen. Japanese martial arts concentrate on the *hara* as the source of strength.

Later, Hawayo Takata changed the order of her hand positions in order to start with the head. It is interesting to note that Orientals traditionally practise meditation with a view to inner calm and self-knowledge, while Westerners have traditionally prized reason and logic and the pursuit of the outer life. Could Hawayo Takata have consciously or unconsciously understood that often the first thing a Westerner needs is to calm the mind?

One of the first people that Hawayo Takata created Reiki master was Beth Gray. She was taught the following set of hand positions by Hawayo Takata; Beth would not change anything that she was given by Hawayo Takata.

As you can see, this set of positions starts on the abdomen. When teaching, Hawayo Takata spoke of the abdomen as the fuelling centre of the body. If this area was right, much else would rebalance. Beth Gray spoke of this area as calming the emotions. Once again, if the emotions are balanced, the body can often right itself.

Some masters and practitioners prefer to keep one of the hands in contact with the body at all times in order to avoid shocking the client with movement (see pages 111–16 on client comfort). Beth's hand movements, as shown below, illustrate two ways of achieving this.

This series of positions is shown with the practitioner working from the left side of the body. Since working from the right side of the body will reverse the hands, I have used the terms 'hand A' and 'hand B'.

Front of torso

Position A1.

Put the middle finger of hand A on the soft spot at the base of the sternum (breastbone). Be careful not to prod or poke. The heel of hand B should touch the tip of the middle finger.

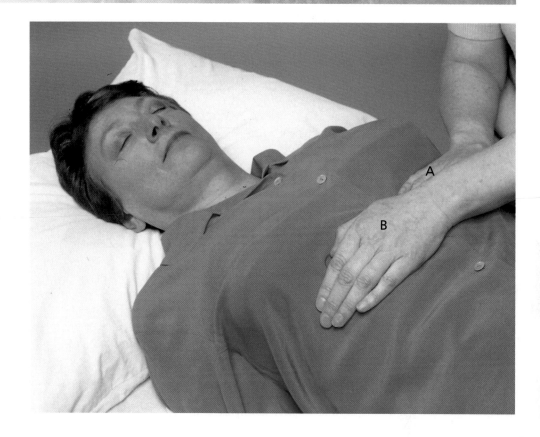

Position A2.

Keeping hand A in position, place hand B immediately below it. Keep the thumbs alongside one another, as shown here, for a more complete coverage of the body.

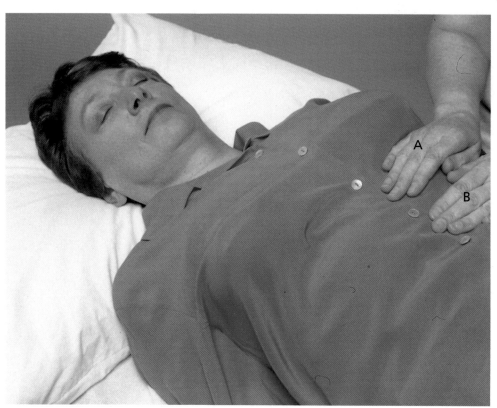

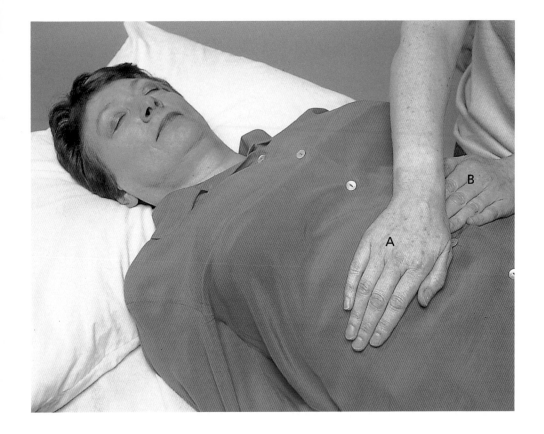

Position A3.
Place the heel of hand A to the middle finger of hand B. When moving position, keep one hand in contact with the body. This reduces the shock of removal that can sometimes be felt by a client.

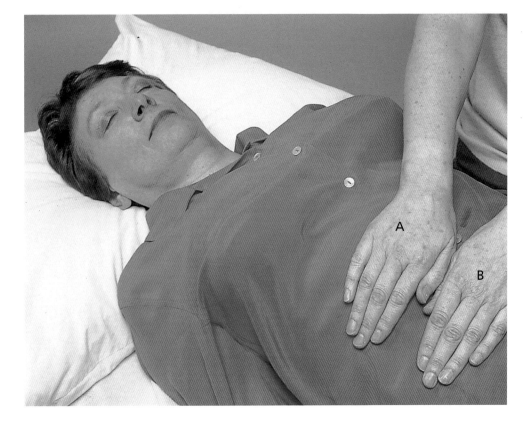

Position A4.
Place hand B immediately below hand A, thumbs touching.

These first four positions treat the emotional centre of the body (the solar plexus). If the person feels nervous, fluttery in the stomach, stressed, angry or abused, this is a good place to start.

Position A5.

Place hand A to the heel of hand B. Continue down the abdomen in this sequence until you reach the lower intestines.

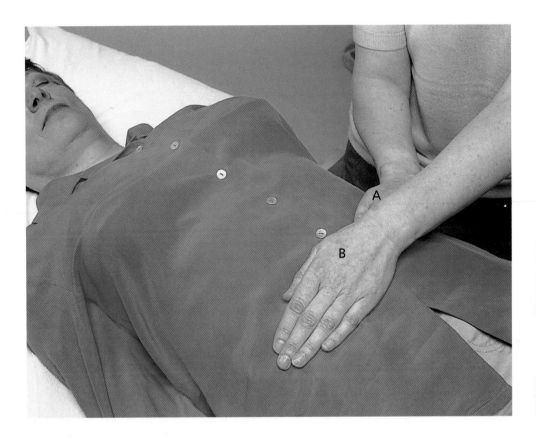

Position B.

On reaching the area contained by the pelvis, place the hands in a 'V' shape, with the heel of hand B resting lightly just inside the pubic bone and the little finger running along the edge of the pelvic bone. Place the fingertips of hand A to the heel of hand B, with the thumb running along the edge of the pelvic bone.

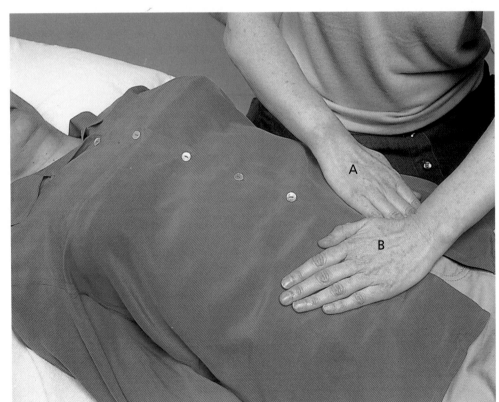

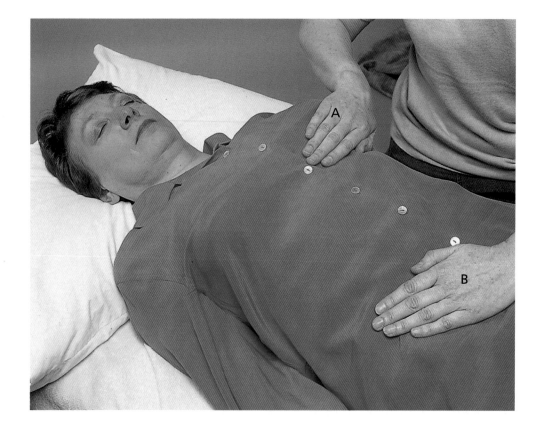

Position C.

Moving back up the body, place hand A on the mid-chest area under the breast, being careful to keep the little finger tucked in so as to avoid the nipple. Place the tip of the middle finger in line with the sternum (breastbone).

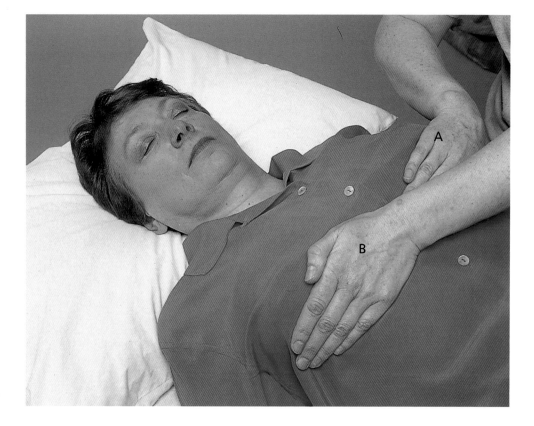

Position D.

Place hand B on the mid-chest area opposite hand A, with the heel of the hand touching the fingertips of hand A. Take care to keep the thumb tucked in to avoid the nipple.

Position E.

Place hand A on the chest, with the thumb above the nipple (again, keep the thumb tucked in).

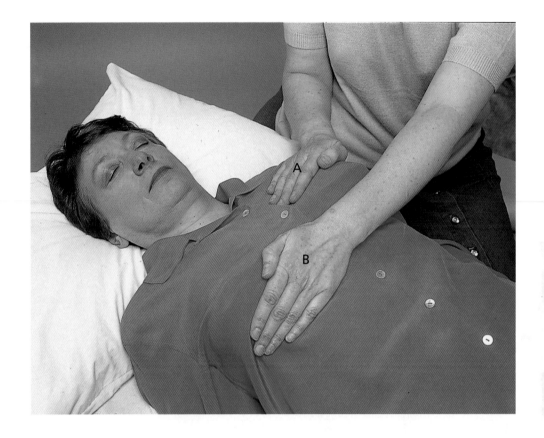

Position F.

Place hand B so that the heel of the hand touches the fingertips of hand A and the little finger rests above the nipple.

The above positions on the breasts are non-intrusive, as the nipples are not touched. Although it is comfortable for women to use them on each other, it may not be advisable for a male practitioner to use them without the presence of a third person.

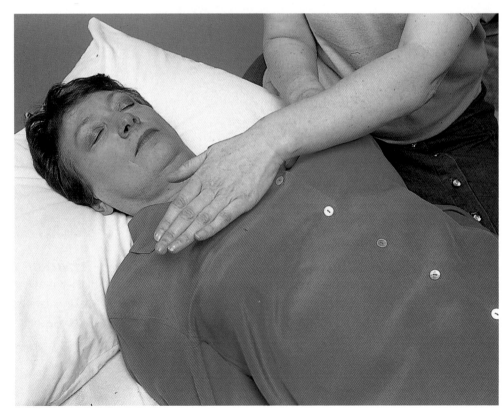

Throat, neck and head

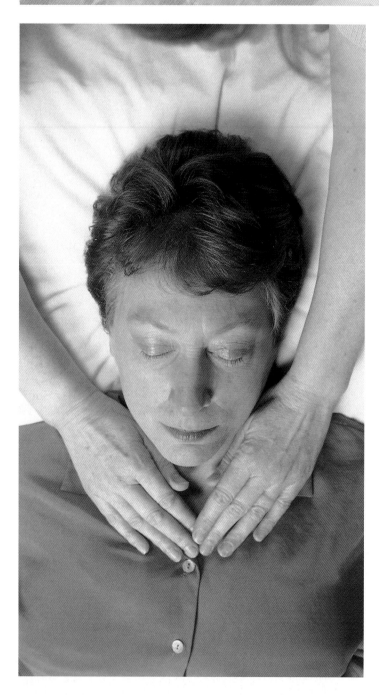

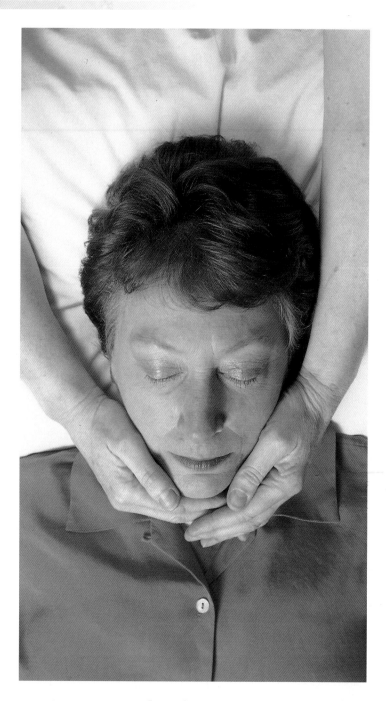

Position G. Base of neck.

Remove hand A from the upper chest and move yourself around to the head of the recipient. Place hand A on the far side of the base of the neck, resting it on the collarbone. Then place hand B on the other collarbone.

Position H. Under chin.

Move one hand and cup it under the chin, just off the body, taking care not to touch the windpipe. Place the other hand likewise immediately below it.

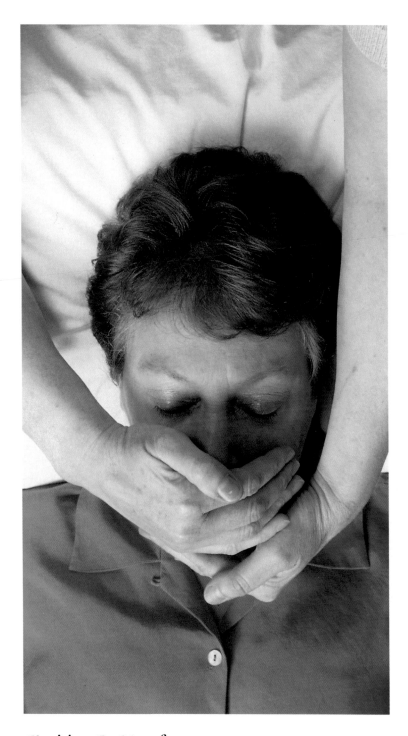

Position I. Mouth.

Bring both hands up to cover the chin and mouth, again holding the hands just off the body. Be careful not to block the nostrils.

Position J. Face.

Move the hands one at a time to lie side by side, with the heels of the hands resting on the eyebrows and the thumbs running along the bridge of the nose. The hands should gently cup the side of the face. Cross the thumbs over each other if the face is small and the hands are touching the ears. Take care not to block the nostrils.

The following three positions show a way of moving the hands over the body that I have observed on several occasions. Again, the hands never leave the body. You can use this method on the torso.

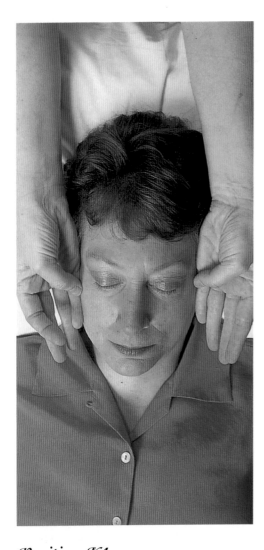 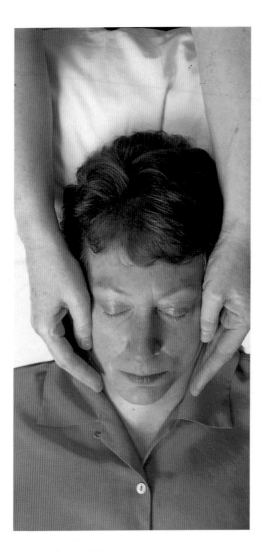 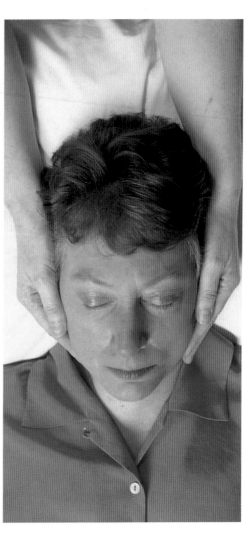

Position K1.
Rolling the hands back . . .
Tucking back your thumbs to the base of your little fingers, place them on the client.

Position K2.
. . . over the ears.
Keeping your thumbs on the same spot, move your hands back over the ears.

Position K3. Ears.
Settle your palms onto the ears.

If you are treating yourself, the order of movement is reversed. The heels of the hands will be on the nostrils. Press the thumbs lightly onto the side of the face, roll your palms over the thumbs, bring the thumbs through and settle the palms onto the ears.

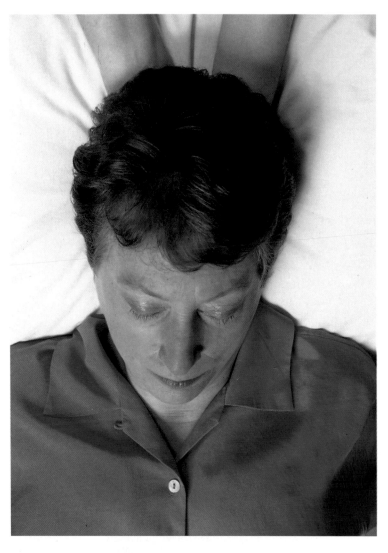

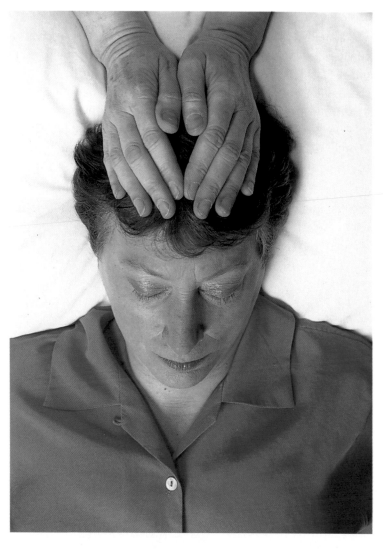

Position L. Back of head.

At this point the recipient may be asleep. If so, gently roll the head onto one of your hands. Slip the other hand under the head and, with the middle finger, feel for the small indentation at the base of the skull where the spine meets the skull. Roll the head gently onto the hand, then slip the other hand underneath.

If the recipient is not asleep, quietly inform them that you are about to turn their head, in which case the client will often either move for you or will raise their head, making the above manoeuvre unnecessary.

Position M. Top of head.

Reverse the above process to remove the hands and then place them onto the crown of the head. You need to sit at this point, because the angle of the wrist would otherwise be too steep.

The hands can either be placed with the fingertips pointing to the face of the recipient, as shown here, or sideways across the top of the head, in which case the thumb of one hand will touch the outer edge of the other.

If you are self-treating using the first of the above alternatives, your fingertips will point to the back of the head.

Treat the back down to the pelvis using positions A1 to A5. Use the 'T' position (one hand across the sacrum, the other down the coccyx) on the base of the spine.

Treating on a chair

There are reasons why it is not always easy to treat a person on a couch. The first and most obvious one is that neither the person giving Reiki nor the receiver has one! Another reason is that space is limited. The room may be too small, you may be giving treatments at an exhibition to help promote your practice or you may be assisting your master at a talk and demonstration. Yet another reason is that the person is uncomfortable lying on a couch. In such cases, you can use a chair or stool.

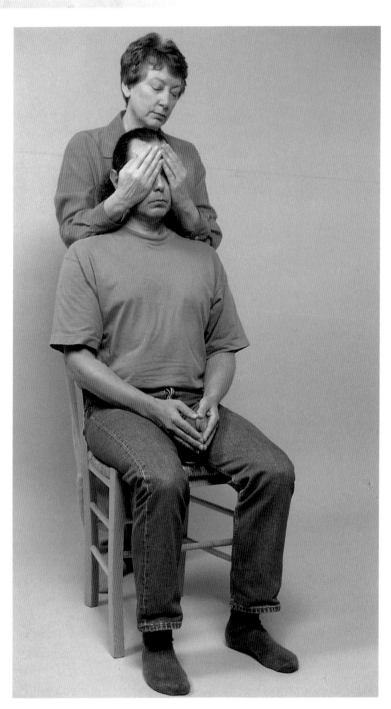

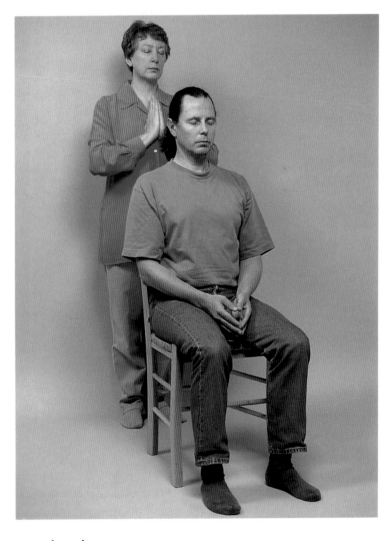

Tuning in.
It is customary to spend a few moments tuning into Reiki before starting a session.

Head.
Hands point upwards for the face and sides of the head. If you put both hands on the back of the head, you will push it forwards, which will be most uncomfortable for both of you. It is therefore customary to put one hand on the forehead and the other across, cradling the back of the skull. It may be more comfortable to treat this latter position standing beside the recipient.

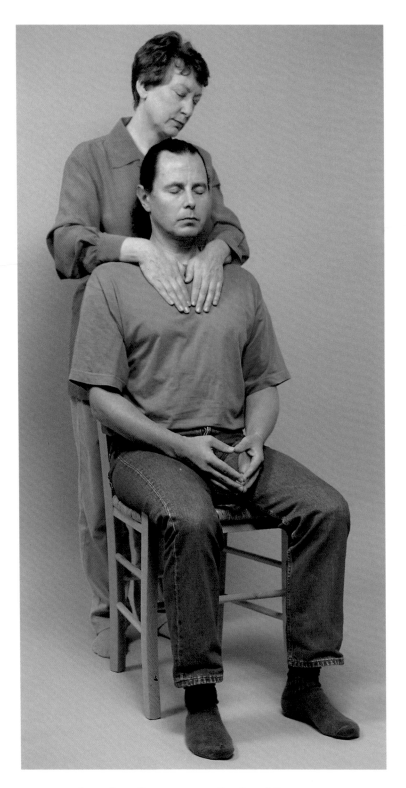

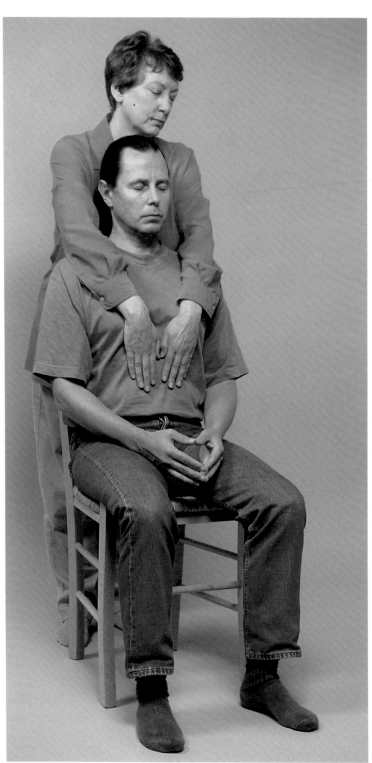

Base of neck, thymus and shoulders.
It is very easy to treat these positions.

Heart and midriff.
You can stretch your hands down to just above the waist unless the person being treated is very large.

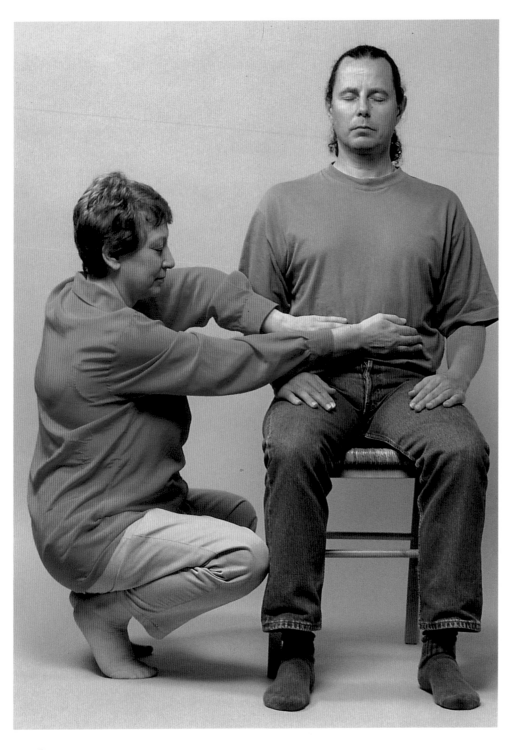

As you can see from the illustrations, you will need to adjust your hand positions and find comfortable ways of adjusting your own body. Treating on a chair has some disadvantages, not least for the healer. It is tiring for your back and also difficult to reach the back of the person being treated.

When treating the back, ask the person at the start of the session whether they would prefer to remain seated, as shown. If they require a lot of attention on the back, they may prefer to sit astride the chair. They need to understand that by the time that you have finished working on the front they will normally be deeply relaxed and unwilling to move. If they choose to sit astride the chair, place a cushion over the top of it to avoid discomfort.

Below waist

You need to find a position that is comfortable to stay in for two to three minutes. You may like to use a low stool or kneel on a cushion.

Extra hand positions

By now it must be obvious that
giving a Reiki treatment is largely a
matter of common sense. You simply
treat the whole body. All of the
organs and glands are covered, as
are the bones, tissues and nerves.
However, there are times when we
want to give ourselves a quick
treatment for a specific acute problem
or to boost a trouble spot.

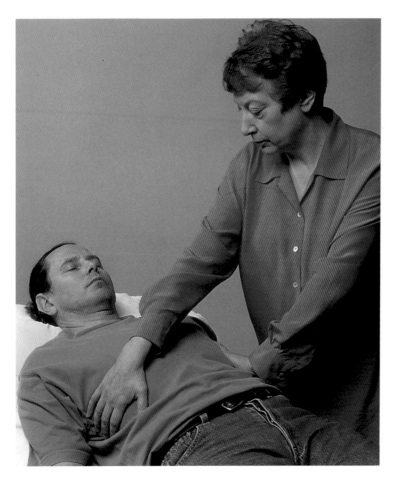

Additional position for lungs and heart.

Infections

If an infection causes cold- or flu-like symptoms, use position 5 (page 36): one hand on the thymus and the other on the throat. This may well remove an accompanying headache without you having to treat the head.

Alternatively, place one hand on the thymus and the other on the spleen. When Reiki has stopped flowing, treat the throat, if it is still sore, and the head, if it feels thick or is aching.

Treat other infections in the same way. For kidney infections, for example, put one hand over the kidneys and the other on the thymus. The thymus is the body's defence gland. Giving Reiki to it can help all immune-system weaknesses and infections, whether it be measles or cancer, a cough or ME.

Lungs and heart

To boost the lungs and heart, place one hand on each side of the body at heart level. You can also move the hands down to the lower ribs to treat the base of the lungs.

After a heart attack, there can be a feeling of constriction in the stomach area. Treat above the waist as necessary. An inverted 'T' position on the head is comforting. It is generally better to treat the constriction below the heart before using the inverted 'T' position, however.

Shock and trauma

You can treat shock and trauma by putting one hand on the thymus and the other on the solar plexus.

When someone has had an accident, they may well be shocked. Place one hand over the injured area an inch or two off the body and the other on the adrenal glands or, if you cannot reach them, the solar plexus.

Shock can kill: when someone is badly burned, for example, it may well be the shock rather than the injury that actually kills them. Giving absent Reiki, or treating the body from a few feet away, can help enormously. If the burns are really severe or life threatening, ask Reiki or your spiritual source to make clear to you whether Reiki treatment would be wise. Reiki intensifies the energy, and the shock may be so deep that it would be kinder not to administer Reiki.

Surgery is traumatic to the body. Reiki can be a real boon in speeding recovery from the surgery and the shock to the system. It also quickens recovery from the effects of the anaesthetic.

You also need to treat the head for shock and trauma.

Unconsciousness

I have mentioned elsewhere that you should not treat someone without his or her permission. But what if they are unconscious? You can ask Reiki or their higher self if it is appropriate. Provided that you are calm and centred, you should be able to feel a definite 'Yes' or 'No'. But at such times you may be so stressed that it is impossible for you to tune into Reiki and ask. If it is inappropriate, it often will not work. If you have a bad feeling about it, stop immediately.

Breasts

For large breasts, mammary infections and tumours, the breasts can be treated separately. Ask permission or explain first. Sandwich each breast, being careful to avoid the nipple.

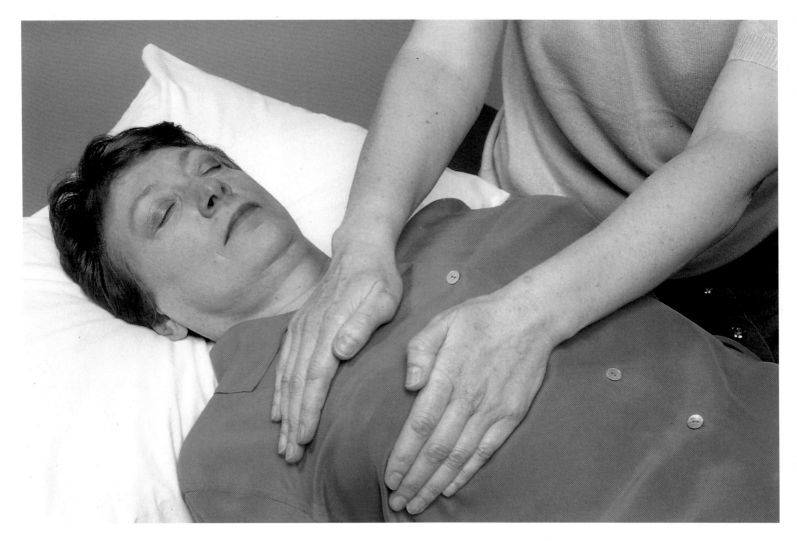

Extra breast treatment.

Physical injury

Broken bones should not receive Reiki until they are set, but you can treat other injuries and ask Reiki that the bones be left untreated.

Sports injuries usually respond well to Reiki. Not long after I started to take clients, I treated my first sports injury. A young woman who was hoping to turn professional had such a bad knee that she had been advised to have surgery. She knew that surgery might permanently weaken the knee, and it was badly swollen and inflamed. After two sessions the leg was so much improved that it precluded the need for surgery. It was a great boost to my confidence.

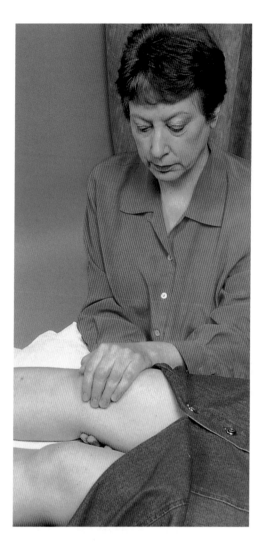

Surgery may be avoided with Reiki.

Sports injuries usually respond well to Reiki.

Spine

The spine must be in good shape for optimum health. I have pointed out several times that hands, especially on the back, should meet in the centre of the body. The spine carries messages to and from the brain and the nerves radiate out from it.

You can give a whole-spinal treatment by placing your hands from the base of the skull down the back, one after the other until you reach the base of the spine. This treatment is helpful for scoliosis, spondylosis, whiplash, slipped discs and all other spinal malfunctions.

For self-treatment of the spine and the back in general, it is possible to treat from the front of the body. This is especially useful when you are treating someone who cannot turn onto his or her front.

People often remark that they can feel Reiki going right into the body.

Arms, legs and hips

So far we have left out the arms and legs. Actually, it is standard practice to treat the arms and legs during group healing. Treatment can be as simple or as intensive as is needed.

Arms

Treating the whole arm helps with the circulation to the arms, arthritis, inflammation and broken bones. Also, the bone marrow produces white blood cells, which fight cancer and aid the immune system.

If you wish to give a general healing to the arm, simply put one hand on the shoulder and, with the other, hold the person's hand. Reiki flows to where it is needed.

If you need to give a more specific treatment, sandwich the appropriate spot between your hands. The lower two photographs on this page show the joints being treated. Suppleness of the joints keeps the body young. If the person has cancer or immune problems, concentrate on the upper arm because the humerus bone is a good producer of white corpuscles. Treating the underarm helps circulation and lymph.

Hips and pelvis

If the hips are out of alignment or are stiff and painful, it can throw the whole body out of kilter. It inevitably puts strain on the pelvis and spine. You can give extra treatment to the hips by sandwiching the joints between your hands. You can also treat them by placing both hands on one side of the body next to the hips or one hand on either side of the body at hip level. These positions ease hip and pelvic rotation. Treat the lower back to release stiffness of muscles.

Treating the whole arm

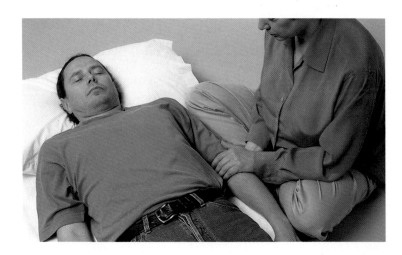

Treating the elbow: place one hand under the elbow, the other on top of it.

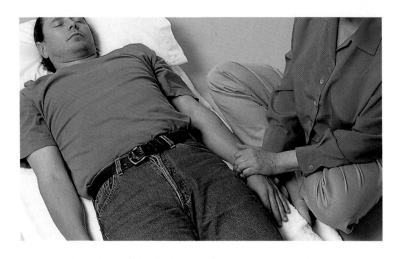

Treating the wrist: sandwich the wrist between your hands.

Legs

For a general leg treatment, put one hand on the groin and the other on the foot.

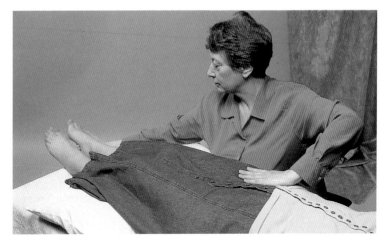

Whole leg, front: one hand at the junction of torso and thigh, the other on the foot. Treats circulation, varicose veins, bones and bone marrow.

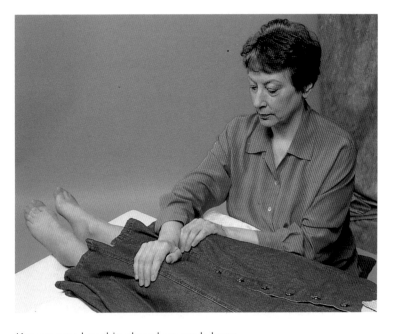

Knees: one hand is placed on each knee.

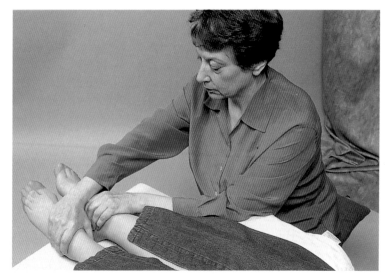

Ankles: one hand is placed on each ankle.

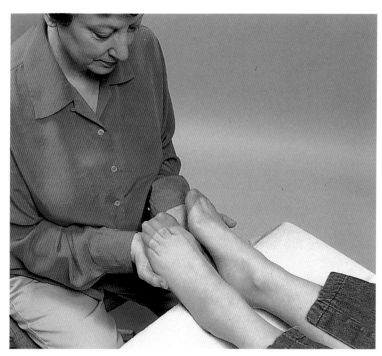

Feet: one hand on each foot. You can run Reiki up the legs from the feet. During group Reiki, one person is often given responsibility for the feet and legs.

Treating the leg joints is usually done on the front of the body. If you need to give a more thorough treatment to a joint, simply sandwich it between your hands. Treat varicose and broken veins by placing the hands on the thighs or on the inside of the thigh and wherever else the treatment is needed.

Sciatica

Sciatic nerve: whole leg.
Sciatica is an uncomfortable problem that is treated on the back of the legs. For a whole-leg treatment, one hand is placed on the sacrum and lower lumbar area of the spine, the other on the heel.

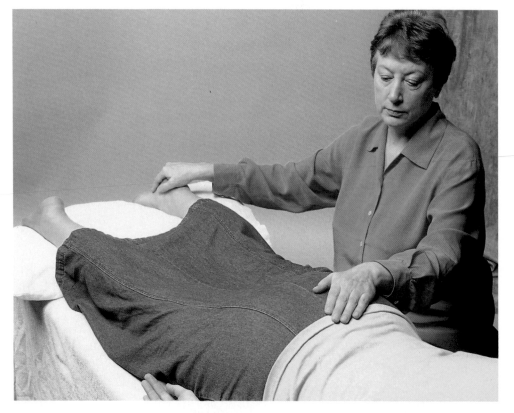

Sciatic nerve: buttock.
More intensive treatment is given by placing the hands down the body in stages, starting with both hands on the buttock, then moving down to the inner thigh and calf muscles (not shown).

These positions are also useful for varicose veins and for grounding.

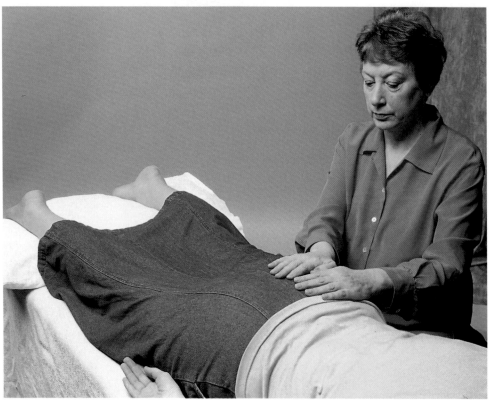

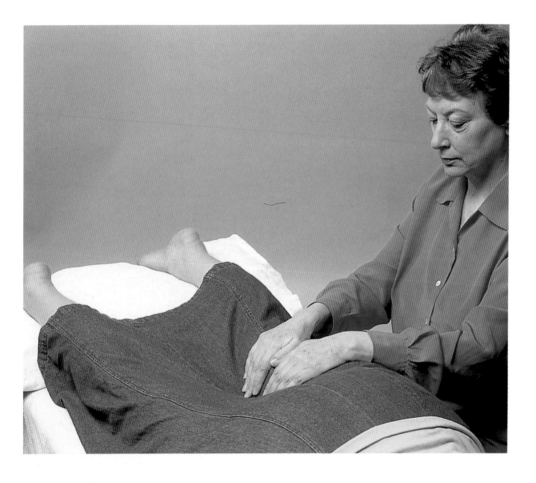

Sciatic nerve: inner thigh.
This position also treats the deep blood vessels and the femur (thigh bone). The femur is the biggest bone in the body. Its bone marrow is an excellent source of white corpuscles, which boost the immune system. Use this position if the person has cancer or ME or shows any other signs of immune-system weakness. You can also treat the thighs on the front of the body.

You can treat the joints from the back. These positions also cover the sciatic nerve.

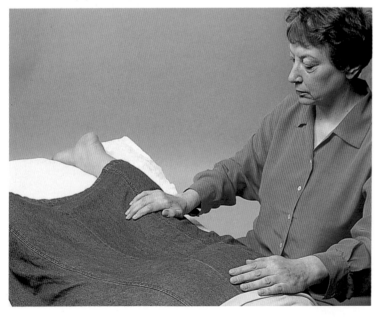

Hip and knee.

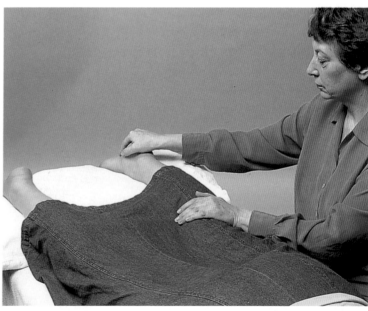

Knee and foot.

Client comfort

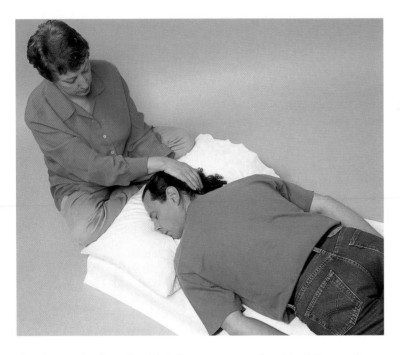

Treating on the floor. Provided that you are comfortable sitting on the floor, it can be quite cosy to treat a friend on sofa cushions or a bedroll

You can light a few candles and some incense and put on your favourite new-age music. Bliss!

It is all very well having a friend around for a Reiki treatment when the bathroom floor is covered with the children's clothes, the spin-dryer is humming and the washing-up is in full view. But if you want to practise professionally, you must be aware of the comfort of your clients. You can, if you wish, decide to attract the more bohemian type, who does not mind the mess!

I have received professional treatments on someone's bed, been covered with an old curtain and surrounded by brick dust and rubble with the explanation that the person had just moved in. I have returned the following week to exactly the same conditions, down to the same rubble in exactly the same place (the middle of the floor). Needless to say, I did not return.

It is not a case of being too fussy: it is simply consideration for your client. Some people will be oblivious to such things, but most people *expect* cleanliness and order. Your treatment room needs to be well aired and clean.

You need to be clean and tidy. Hands and clothes smelling of cigarettes and nicotine-stained fingers are to be avoided. Be aware of strong-smelling perfume and aftershave. People are very open during Reiki and much more sensitive to such things. Make sure that your hands in particular are clean, with clean fingernails, and smell of nothing or a gentle, natural soap.

You may love the smell of incense or scented candles. Many people do not. Make sure that the room is relatively free of such smells before you meet with a client for the first time. Either ask them what they would like or make it a policy not to use incense and scented candles.

Similarly, please check that your client likes background music and, if so, ask what kind they would prefer. Again, you may prefer not to play music.

When you are first starting out, it is acceptable to treat on the floor, but you will soon need to get a couch. Nowadays, so many people are training in therapies that you may be able to find a cheap, second-hand couch.

You need to decide upon which height is suitable for you. You may be small and wish to sit while giving treatments or may be tall and wish to stand. Some couches have adjustable legs, but these are more expensive.

When you are settling your client on to the couch, ask them if they are comfortable. They may prefer two pillows under their head. A pillow under the knees frequently takes some strain off the spine, and when they turn over you can put a pillow under their ankles.

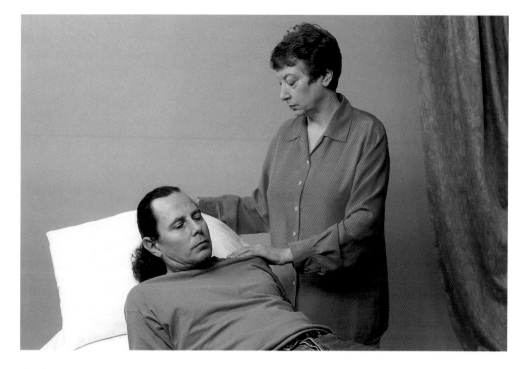

Check whether your client needs an extra pillow.

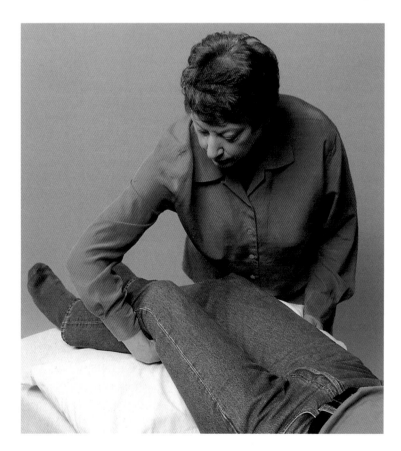

Putting a pillow under the knees.

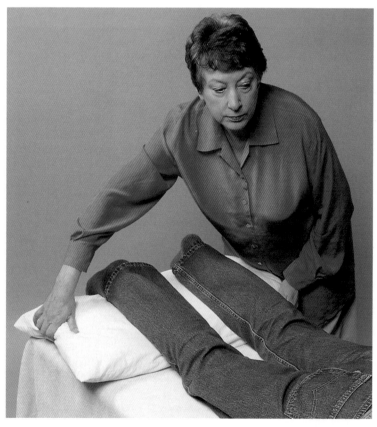

When your client is lying face down, put a pillow under their ankles.

Some couches have face-holes. When the client turns over, you need to open the face-hole for them quickly. It is usual to wrap something round the face-hole. You can roll up a towel and wrap it around the face-hole or you can buy a padded face ring. Many people prefer not to use face-holes.

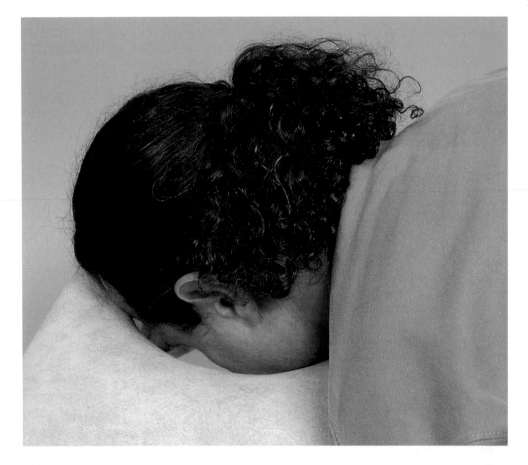

Using a face-hole.

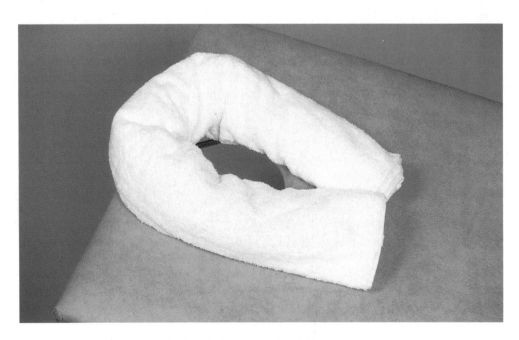

You can wrap a towel around a face-hole for added cushioning.

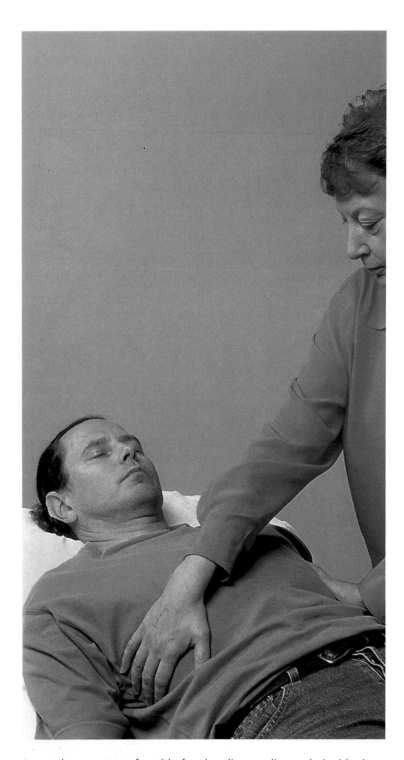

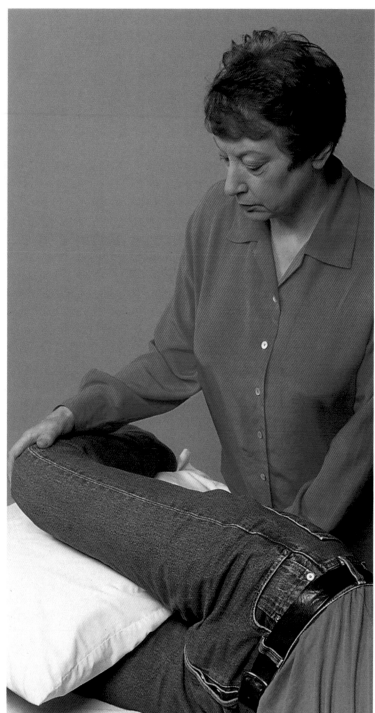

It may be more comfortable for the client to lie on their side, in which case you may need to prop them in place with pillows or place a pillow between the knees.

It may be more comfortable for the client to lie on their side, in which case you may need to prop them in place with pillows or place a pillow between the knees.

When your client is comfortably settled on the couch and you have discussed what, if anything, they wish to have the treatment for, spend a few moments centring yourself and tuning into Reiki.

There are a few places on the body that are very vulnerable and sensitive. These inlcude the face, throat and breasts.

When you give a treatment, normally your first position is the face. Lower your hands gently onto it, or stay an inch or two off it.

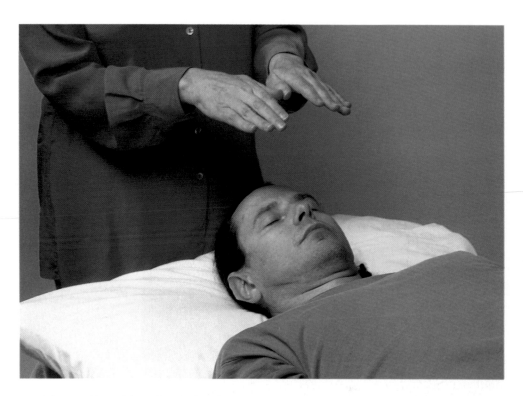

Your first position with a client is their face . . .

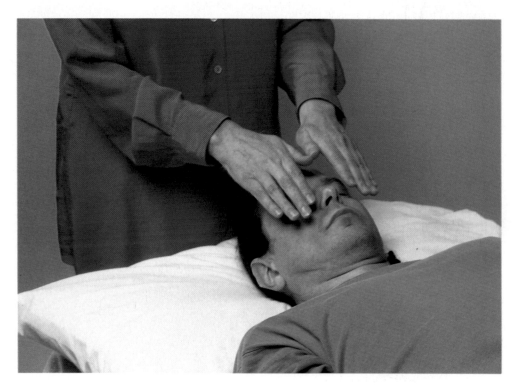

. . . make sure that you approach it gently.

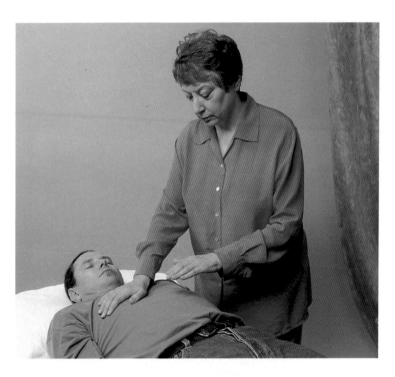

Your client will usually become deeply relaxed and open very quickly. If you knock your client or tickle them, they may not be able to relax completely. When you move around their body, be careful not to knock the table. If you do knock or tickle someone, always apologise. This makes them aware that you have realised and helps them to relax and trust you. As you move from position to position, continue to be aware of approaching the body gently. Some masters and practitioners prefer to keep one hand in contact at all times.

Tell your client when you have finished the treatment. Allow them time to return to a grounded state before leaving your premises.

When you move positions, avoid knocking the couch.

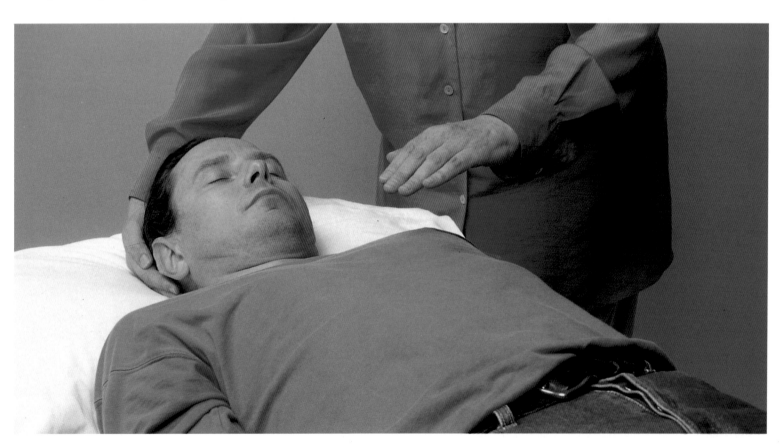

You may prefer to keep one hand in contact as you move.

Further uses

There is no limit to Reiki. It comes from pure being. It is infinite intelligence. It is pure love. Each time that you use it you pour light and love into yourself and your recipient. Reiki opens up your heart and fills you with love and life energy. You begin to glow. Reiki is very bonding. You can meet someone from far away, and, on discovering that you both have Reiki, feel an instant connection.

Plants respond to Reiki.

Reiki is transforming you every time that you use it. Like water on a stone, it wears away your resistance and your limitations. It transforms your consciousness and your body. Habits die, resentments are forgotten and you begin to look younger! Reiki not only transforms your inner world, it heals your connection to the outer world.

The following are a few ways in which you can use Reiki.

Animals

Many animals love Reiki. Some people learn Reiki specifically to use on animals. I had the privilege of attending a stable recently. It was fascinating to experience the different personalities of the horses and to use Reiki to help their problems. Some of them had been badly mishandled before arriving at the stable, and the owner was concerned that some animals would have to be put down. One magnificent horse was so frightened that he would only allow the head of the stables to ride him. It was a wonderful experience to approach the horse from several feet away, with my hands directing Reiki to his body, and slowly to move closer without violating his space until I could touch him. It took 20 minutes.

Plants

Plants love Reiki. Remember the explanation of the meaning of Reiki on page 16. Rice is actually included in the Reiki *kanji* (see page 15).

When a plant is looking sick, or you have neglected it, you can give it Reiki. You can give Reiki to boost the life force of trees and the earth. You can give Reiki to the garden by directing your hands towards it. You might like to give Reiki to seeds before planting them, or to cuttings to encourage the growth of roots. If you are a farmer, you can direct your hands towards your fields and livestock. If you learn Level II Reiki, much of this can be done quickly and easily.

Machinery

Scientists will laugh outright in sheer derision at the stories that I could tell about machinery. Many a car mechanic has shaken his head in disbelief upon being presented with a vehicle that should not be moving; radios and tape recorders have defied logic.

I was recently in the desert with three other people. We were driving through a mountain pass on a rocky and remote road. Suddenly, while trying to get up a slope, the car stalled. The wheels became lodged and each attempt to clear the car only dug us in deeper. We all got out of the vehicle and did our best to remedy the situation. Nothing worked.

Suddenly I had an idea. 'Three of us have Reiki. Why don't we use it?' We all applied our second-degree mental use of Reiki.

Unbelievably, we had hardly finished when a group of men walked into view. We were a little apprehensive. Would they be friendly? Would they help us?

They grasped the situation immediately. Without a word, one of them got into the driver's seat, started the car and roared off over the hill. Our reaction was a mixture of relief that the car was free and apprehension – would we ever see our vehicle again?

We need not have worried. At the top of the hill our car – and our helpful driver – were waiting. It was only later that we discovered that the four-wheel drive, essential for driving in such conditions, had broken.

Another car story happened in more mundane surroundings. I was crawling through a traffic jam on a hot Saturday afternoon when the car stalled. With help, I pushed it to the kerb and waited for a while. When the car still did not start, I put my free hand on the bonnet and used my second-degree symbols.

Within minutes I spotted an AA van crawling towards me. As it drew level, I asked the driver if he was on a call. He replied that he wasn't. I said 'You are now!' He lifted the bonnet and discovered the problem. I would never have got home without him. Reiki had saved me a long, hot wait.

Food

For me, one of the enjoyable aspects of a Reiki class is lunch. Those who hate cooking bring something prepacked from the supermarket or a hunk of bread and some cheese, and those who like cooking treat us to a favourite recipe. Then we all gather to eat.

Before we start, I tell everyone that we are going to give Reiki to the food. They are interested and surprised. I invite them to think about the processes that the food has gone through: the application of herbicides and pesticides, cooking and packaging, transportation and handling. Reiki restores the energy of the food that has been lost since it was harvested.

I automatically give Reiki to my food. In a restaurant, you can surreptitiously apply it to your food either by leaning on your elbows and putting your hands over the plate or holding the sides of the plate with the palms of your hands. Nobody need ever know.

Surroundings

Many masters give Reiki to the room in which they are about to teach or practise. This builds the energy before the class treatment starts.

In short, in applying Reiki in your life you are limited only by your imagination.

Points to ponder

A Reiki practitioner is not an alternative to the medical profession, but a complement to it. Do not attempt to diagnose or otherwise undermine what a qualified physician is doing or can do for their patient. You should never tell someone to refrain from medication. But you should make it clear to your clients that dosages should be checked after treatment with Reiki.

Reiki does not always work. There can be many reasons for this. One reason may be that the person would benefit more from a different therapy. When someone asks to book a session for the first time, if it does not feel right, trust your intuition. Ask them why they chose you, use your knowledge of therapies and local therapists, tell them courteously what you feel and suggest what *does* feel right. Provided that you are sensitive about it, they will respect you for it.

Another reason why Reiki may not work is that the person consciously or subconsciously does not wish to be well. There are many reasons for this. The person may like the attention that he or she gains by being ill or may possibly be too heartbroken to wish to live.

A third reason is that there may be a lesson to learn, and until it has been learnt the person cannot be healed. We cannot heal people just because we want to be healed and because we have Reiki. There are many spiritual tests along the way.

Exchange of energy

One of the interesting facets of Reiki is that there must be a fair exchange of energy for it. Hawayo Takata's version of Dr Usui's life highlights this. He was reputed to have given Reiki free to beggars and to have found them honest work until he discovered that one of them had gone back to begging because it was easier. Dr Usui was so upset by this ingratitude that he resolved never again to give Reiki free.

Shortly after Hawayo Takata became a Reiki master, one of her neighbours asked to receive Level I Reiki. Because Hawayo was grateful to her friends and family for their support, she gave her neighbour Level I Reiki free. But every time that her neighbour's children became sick or had a fall she would come running to Hawayo for Reiki. Hawayo became quite angry and asked her neighbour why she came to her when she could give Reiki herself. 'You are the master', she replied. Then Hawayo remembered the story of Dr Usui.

She also recalled that Dr Hayashi had told her never to give Reiki free because it would not be appreciated. He was right. Her neighbour never used it.

When her sister asked to be taught Reiki, Hawayo told her that she must pay. She was very offended, but her husband agreed with Hawayo and her sister later used Reiki constantly, prospered and was full of gratitude.

Friends and family usually exchange enough small favours among themselves to make giving and receiving Reiki a pleasure. But you do need to be aware that sometimes a family member or friend may be more inclined to take than give. One of my students told me that although her 12-year-old daughter was asking for Reiki, she felt reluctant to give it. I asked her what her daughter did around the house. She replied that her daughter was no help at all. I invited her to look at the fact that there was no exchange of energy and suggested that she give Reiki in exchange for her daughter doing some chores.

Ask permission

Do not try to push someone into receiving Reiki or to give it to him or her without permission. A long while ago I received a salutary lesson. I used my Level II distant healing, along with a very powerful crystal, to send healing to someone who I knew was going through a bad time. An hour later the person stormed in demanding to know what I had been doing. I had blocked an inner process that she had been doing and she had picked up that I was the cause.

Dying

Sooner or later it will be time for a person to leave their body. It can be a privilege to see someone through such a time. Although nothing is going to take away the pain of bereavement completely, Reiki is a wonderful way of relieving the fear and distress of all concerned. Be aware that when someone who you have treated dies, neither you nor Reiki have failed.

Reiki is full of love.
It opens the heart to life.
Reiki is full of wisdom.
It is attempting to teach you all the time.
Listen to it.
Reiki is full of strength.
It is life force.

Level II

After you have been doing Reiki for a few months, you may feel drawn to taking Level II. When you learn Level II, you begin to use Reiki consciously. You are learning to take responsibility for yourself and your life. Reiki II is more powerful psychologically. It is the clearing level where you learn how to tackle your emotions. You learn to wield your tools. You learn how to give distant healing and how to use Reiki on relationships and events. Because it can be abused, Level II is not given to children under 16.

If you have done Level II Reiki, you can apply it mentally in all sorts of ways. You can treat yourself or another with the intention of healing a specific attitude or feeling, for gaining insight into a trigger point or an emotional issue or for help with a weakness. Here are a few examples.

You may be aware that you are critical of others or you may be self-critical. You can apply your second-degree techniques to help you to release this attitude or to understand why you have it.

Perhaps certain things cause you to cry. What is the trigger? Ask Reiki and apply your techniques.

You may be always late. Why?

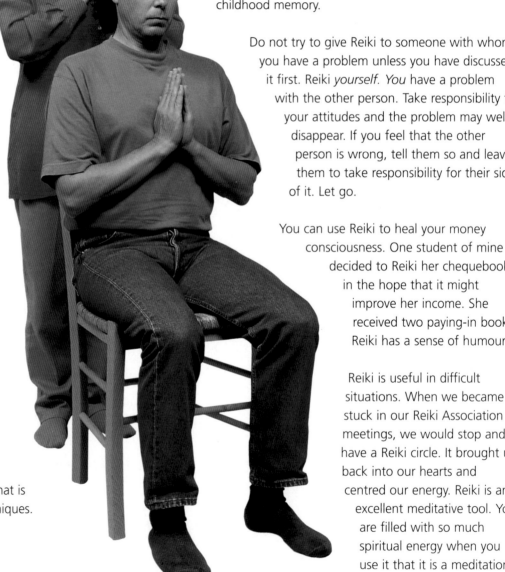

When you do a Level II class, you learn how to use Reiki on events and situations. For instance, you can give Reiki to a job interview beforehand or to help while house-hunting. You can use it to heal your feelings about a past event, perhaps a relationship break-up or a bad childhood memory.

Do not try to give Reiki to someone with whom you have a problem unless you have discussed it first. Reiki *yourself*. *You* have a problem with the other person. Take responsibility for your attitudes and the problem may well disappear. If you feel that the other person is wrong, tell them so and leave them to take responsibility for their side of it. Let go.

You can use Reiki to heal your money consciousness. One student of mine decided to Reiki her chequebook in the hope that it might improve her income. She received two paying-in books. Reiki has a sense of humour!

Reiki is useful in difficult situations. When we became stuck in our Reiki Association meetings, we would stop and have a Reiki circle. It brought us back into our hearts and centred our energy. Reiki is an excellent meditative tool. You are filled with so much spiritual energy when you use it that it is a meditation in itself.

Level III

Level III is the teaching degree. The trainee assists the master in classes and sharing groups, at exhibitions, talks and demonstrations, and, as their training progresses, may take responsibility for some aspects. The trainee is taught the full history of Reiki as far as the master knows it, and is made aware of developments within Reiki. The form and structure of classes is taught, along with the initiations. The student is given guidelines on how to set up classes and venues and generally find students. The trainee organises classes for the master as part of their training and other assignments may also be given.

During this time the trainee is growing into the energy of becoming a master.

Some masters wait until the last day of training to give their students the form of initiations and the Level III initiation. Personally, I prefer to give the initiation at, or near, the beginning of training. It can cause big changes, and I prefer to be available to support the trainee.

But learning the practicalities of teaching Reiki are only half of the equation.

Reiki is a transformational path. While the new master may receive much encouragement and lots of light, it will not be long before the spiritual training begins to deepen, provided that the student is ready for the energy of Level III.

Level III is a full-enlightenment path. As the master develops, the tests become harder. All of one's fears have to be faced and all of the spiritual tests must be passed before enlightenment can be fully gained: courage, compassion, wisdom, integrity and honesty, to name but a few qualities.

But, if you listen, Reiki will guide you all the way.

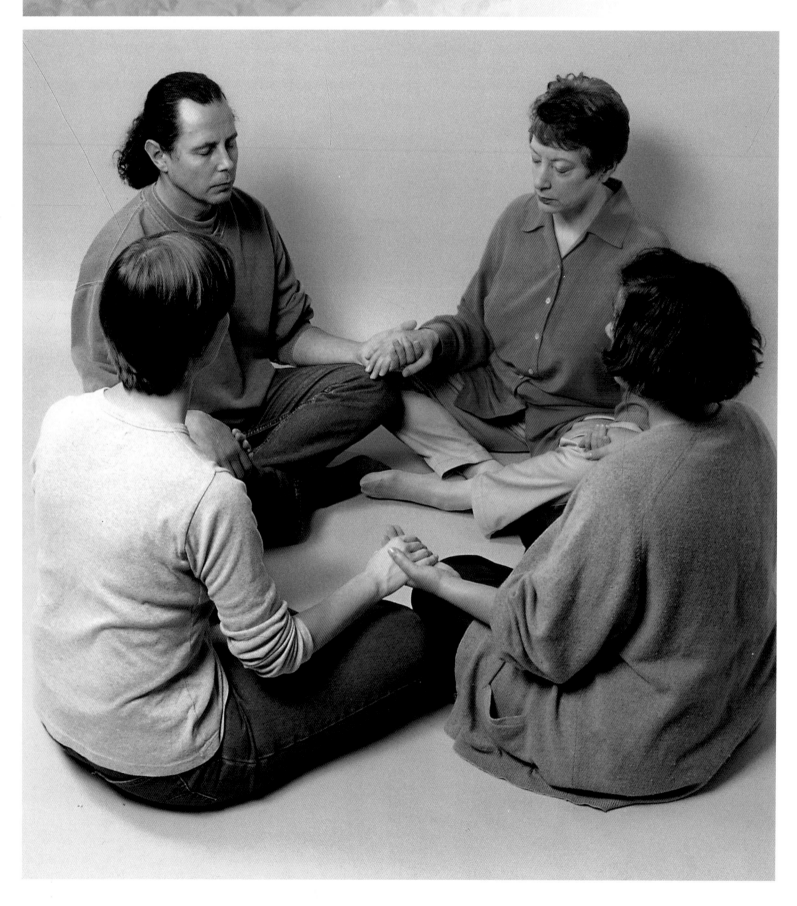

When Hawayo Takata died, she left as her successor her granddaughter, Phyllis Furumoto. Some of Takata's masters gathered around Phyllis, who was very young, and formed an association called the Reiki Alliance. You can find information about it on the Internet.

Nowadays, Reiki has become mixed with different energies. It can be learnt very quickly, often in different forms, but, confusingly, is still called Reiki.

If you wish to experience Reiki, you will find that many clinics have a Reiki practitioner. 'New-age' shops will probably know someone in the area and may have some cards or leaflets or perhaps sell magazines that carry advertisements for Reiki.

You can find yearbooks for complementary medicine that contain addresses and contact numbers in your local library.

If you wish to learn Reiki, first attend exhibitions, talks, demonstrations and Reiki sharing groups or talk to some masters on the phone before deciding on who is to teach you. Ask them how long they have been doing Reiki, how long their training lasted, what their fees are and get a feel for them. If you feel attracted to a master, ask to meet them, and perhaps have a treatment. Take your time until you feel that you have found the right teacher for you. Sometimes you just know instantly.

If you wish to become a practitioner of Reiki in the UK, you would be advised to contact the Confederation of Healing Organisations or the National Federation of Spiritual Healers for guidelines on what is required for professional practice by law, the British Medical Association and other interested bodies.

The Reiki Association publishes a guide to teachers and practitioners. According to its constitution, the association is open to any form of Reiki, so it does not guarantee the standard of the practitioners and masters on its lists, but it does give guidelines on relevant questions to ask.

Wherever you wish to teach or practise, it is wise to check local law. Some states or countries forbid treatment of certain parts of the body without the relevant qualification. Some require all practitioners to have specific qualifications for any bodywork.

Glossary

Chakra

Vortex of subtle energy. Chakras are situated throughout the body. The seven major chakras are situated along the spine and in the head.

Hara

The abdomen, centre of focus for Japanese martial arts. The centre of the *hara* is just below the navel.

Holistic

Pertaining to the whole person, body, mind and spirit, bringing into wholeness.

Kanji

Japanese writing in the form of pictograms.

Shaman

Priest.

Index

Credits and Acknowledgements

I am indebted to Reiki Master Jennifer McDiarmid for the inclusion of Hawayo Takata's hand positions as taught to Beth Gray with whom Jennifer learnt Level I Reiki in May 1985 and Level II Reiki in November 1985.

My grateful thanks to Jennifer and Reiki Master Hjalmar Jonsson for modelling the photos and for their love and support during the whole project.

Hjalmar received Level I from Paula Horan in 1989 and Level II from Gudrun Oladottir, Iceland's first Reiki master, in 1990.

Both Hjalmar and Jennifer did their master training with me and both were board members of the Reiki Association.

Illustrations and artwork on pages 2, 6, 14, 15, 24, 27, 45, 90, 117, 119 by Pauline Cherrett.

Photograph on page 20 by Craig Coussins.

Guildford College
Learning Resource Centre

Please return on or before the last date shown
This item may be renewed by telephone unless overdue

1 6 MAY 2005		
1 0 JUN 2005		
─ 9 JUN 2006		
1 3 MAR 2013		

Class: 615.852 WIN

Title: Reiki

Author: WINSER Charmian